The Digital Nomad ڒ Handbook

Freedom, Flexibility, and Thriving Anywhere in the World

Revised, September 2025

Alex Bugeja

Table of Contents

Introduction

Imagine waking up not to the sound of a blaring alarm clock demanding you begin your commute, but to the gentle lapping of waves on a Thai beach. Your office for the day is a rustic beachfront café, your colleagues a global network of professionals connected by Wi-Fi, and your afternoon break involves a quick swim in the turquoise sea. This isn't a scene from a far-fetched movie or a fleeting two-week vacation. For a rapidly growing number of people, this is simply Tuesday. This is the world of the digital nomad, a lifestyle that untethers work from a specific geographical location, offering in its place a potent cocktail of freedom, flexibility, and global exploration.

The allure is undeniable. Who wouldn't want to trade a cramped cubicle for a co-working space in Lisbon, or a monotonous daily commute for a weekend exploring ancient ruins in Mexico? The glossy images on social media paint a picture of perpetual adventure, of laptops open against stunning backdrops, and of a life lived on one's own terms. This vision, full of personal and professional growth opportunities, is a powerful motivator, promising an escape from the conventional 9-to-5 grind and a chance to design a life that aligns with a passion for travel and new experiences. It speaks to a deep-seated desire to see the world, not as a tourist rushing through a checklist, but as a temporary local, truly immersing oneself in different cultures.

However, the reality of this lifestyle is far more nuanced than a perfectly curated Instagram feed. Behind every breathtaking sunset photo is the often-unseen hustle: the scramble for reliable internet, the challenge of navigating complex visa regulations, and the persistent hum of loneliness that can accompany a life in constant motion. The same freedom that makes the lifestyle so attractive can also lead to a blurred line between work and leisure, where the pressure to be constantly available can lead to burnout. This handbook is born from that duality. It is designed to be your guide through both the dazzling highs and the inevitable, character-building lows of the digital nomad journey.

This is not a book that will sell you a fantasy. Instead, it is a practical, no-nonsense manual for building a sustainable and fulfilling life as a location-independent professional. We will strip away the romanticism to reveal the sturdy framework required to make this dream a reality. The goal is to equip you with the tools, strategies, and realistic expectations needed not just to survive, but to truly thrive, anywhere in the world. It's about understanding that freedom and flexibility are not simply handed to you; they are earned through meticulous planning, unwavering self-discipline, and a healthy dose of resilience.

So, what exactly is a digital nomad? The term, once niche, has entered the mainstream lexicon, but its meaning can still be fluid. At its core, a digital nomad is an individual who leverages technology to work remotely while traveling. They are not on a permanent vacation. They are professionals—freelancers, entrepreneurs, and increasingly, full-time employees—who have simply swapped a fixed office for a mobile one. Their work is performed through laptops, smartphones, and a crucial reliance on internet access, allowing them to perform their jobs from cafes, libraries, or dedicated co-working spaces across the globe.

The digital nomad community is not a monolith. It comprises a diverse range of professions, from programmers and graphic designers to writers, marketers, and consultants. The common thread that binds them is not their job title, but their commitment to a location-independent lifestyle. This distinguishes them from traditional remote workers who, while not tied to a central office, tend to maintain a stable home base in one geographic area. The nomad, by contrast, embraces mobility, often moving every few months, or even weeks, to explore new cities and countries.

This lifestyle choice represents a fundamental re-evaluation of the traditional relationship between work and life. It prioritizes experiences over material possessions and autonomy over the rigid structures of corporate life. The pioneers of this movement were often freelancers and tech entrepreneurs who forged their own path in the early 2000s. However, what was once a fringe movement has now become a viable and aspirational career path for millions, a testament to a broader cultural shift in what people seek from their professional lives. The focus has moved away from simply climbing a career ladder to building a life that offers a more holistic sense of fulfillment.

This isn't just a generational whim. While the lifestyle is popular among millennials, workers of all ages are embracing this mode of work. The motivations are varied but often circle back to a core set of desires: escaping the rat race, achieving a better work-life balance, and gaining the ability to pursue personal interests and hobbies that a conventional job might not accommodate. It is a conscious choice to design a life where work serves as an enabler of adventure, rather than an obstacle to it.

The rise of the digital nomad is not an accident of history but the result of a powerful confluence of technological advancement and a seismic shift in workplace culture. The very possibility of this lifestyle is built on a foundation of modern technology. The proliferation of high-speed internet, the advent of cloud computing, and the development of sophisticated collaboration tools like Slack and Zoom have effectively dismantled the geographic barriers that once chained work to a physical office. These tools make it possible to communicate and collaborate seamlessly across continents and time zones.

Technological innovation alone, however, was not enough. The true catalyst for the explosion in digital nomadism was the global pandemic. The sudden, worldwide shift to remote work forced companies to confront and overcome their long-held resistance to telecommuting. This mass experiment proved on an unprecedented scale that productivity was not tied to physical presence. As a result, many organizations have adopted permanent remote or hybrid work policies, inadvertently opening the door for their employees to explore a location-independent life.

This "new normal" of work has legitimized a lifestyle that was once seen as unconventional. The pandemic prompted a collective re-evaluation of life's priorities, with many people realizing they craved more flexibility, autonomy, and a better balance between their personal and professional lives. The freedom from the daily commute and the rigid 9-to-5 schedule gave people a taste of a different way of living, and for many, there was no going back. This cultural reset has been a primary driver behind the significant growth in the number of people identifying as digital nomads.

Furthermore, the world has begun to adapt to this growing movement. Recognizing the economic benefits that these traveling professionals can bring, dozens of countries have started offering "digital nomad visas." These specialized visas simplify the legal complexities of living and working abroad for extended periods, providing a clear legal framework that was previously a major hurdle. This growing infrastructure, from visa programs to the proliferation of co-working spaces and coliving arrangements, signals that digital nomadism is not a fleeting trend but a durable and evolving feature of the future of work.

This handbook is designed to be your comprehensive guide, a trusted companion on what can be an incredibly rewarding, yet equally challenging, journey. It is structured to walk you through every stage of the process, from the initial decision-making to the long-term strategies for creating a sustainable nomadic life. We will move beyond the inspirational platitudes and dive deep into the practical realities of what it takes to succeed. This book is a roadmap, meticulously charted to help you navigate the complex terrain of location independence.

Our journey will begin with the fundamentals. We'll explore the mindset required for success, focusing on the critical importance of flexibility, resilience, and self-discipline. We will then delve into the "how" of earning an income on the road, breaking down the primary paths of freelancing, remote employment, and entrepreneurship. You'll learn about the in-demand skills that are most compatible with this lifestyle and discover actionable strategies for landing remote work, building a compelling portfolio, and crafting proposals that win clients.

From there, we will tackle the logistical bedrock of nomadic life. These are the crucial, often overlooked, details that can make or break your experience. We will cover the essentials of financial planning, from creating a robust budget to managing savings and investments while living a mobile life. We will demystify the complexities of taxes and international banking, and provide a clear-eyed guide to navigating the labyrinth of visas and legal requirements. These chapters are designed to remove the guesswork and provide you with a clear, actionable framework for managing the administrative side of your life.

Finally, we will explore the art and science of the lifestyle itself. You will find practical advice on everything from the art of packing light to choosing the right gear and digital tools for your mobile office. We'll examine how to select your destinations, find suitable accommodation, and maintain a reliable internet connection. Crucially, we will address the human side of this journey: how to build a global community, combat loneliness, and prioritize your health and wellness on the go. We will discuss productivity strategies for working across time zones, the importance of cultural etiquette, and how to handle the inevitable challenges that arise on the road.

This book is for the dreamers who are ready to become doers. It is for the aspiring nomad who is feeling overwhelmed and unsure where to start. It is for the current remote worker who is curious about taking their job on the road but is nervous about the logistics. It is also for the seasoned nomad who is looking for ways to optimize their lifestyle, scale their career, and ensure the long-term sustainability of their journey. This is a guide for anyone who believes that work should support their life, not define it.

However, this book is not for those seeking a quick escape or an easy path. The digital nomad lifestyle is not a permanent vacation; it is a conscious and often demanding integration of work and travel. It requires a strong work ethic, exceptional time management skills, and a high degree of personal accountability. If you are looking for a magic formula that promises wealth without effort or adventure without challenges, you will not find it here. Success in this realm is not about finding shortcuts; it's about building a solid foundation of skills, systems, and mindset.

This handbook is an investment in your freedom. It is a compilation of the hard-won lessons, practical strategies, and essential knowledge you need to turn the dream of a location-independent life into your reality. The path ahead is not always easy, but it is filled with unparalleled opportunities for growth, discovery, and connection. The world is waiting, your office can be anywhere, and your adventure is ready to begin. This guide is the first step on that journey, providing the clarity and confidence you need to take the leap.

CHAPTER ONE: The Digital Nomad Revolution: Redefining Work and Travel

For the better part of a century, the blueprint for a successful professional life was remarkably consistent. It involved a college degree, a steady job at a reputable company, and a decades-long climb up the corporate ladder. The goal was stability, symbolized by a mortgage, a company pension, and a predictable, structured existence. Work happened in a designated building, between the hours of nine and five, and life—real life, it was often felt—was something that happened on evenings, weekends, and during a cherished two-week vacation each year. This model was the bedrock of the industrial and post-industrial economy, a rigid framework that defined not just our careers, but our identities and aspirations.

The digital nomad revolution represents the most profound challenge to that framework in generations. It is not merely a new way to work or a trendy way to travel; it is a fundamental re-imagining of the relationship between our professional and personal lives. This revolution suggests that work does not have to be a place you go, but something you do. It proposes that a life rich in global experience is not something to be saved for retirement, but something that can be integrated into your most productive years. It dismantles the old binary of "work" versus "life" and blends them into a fluid, location-independent existence.

This shift didn't materialize overnight. Its roots can be traced back to the burgeoning internet culture of the late 1990s, a time of dial-up modems and digital frontiers. Early pioneers, often tech-savvy freelancers and iconoclastic entrepreneurs, began to experiment with the idea of a mobile office. They were the trailblazers, patching together a working life from internet cafes in cities like Chiang Mai and Berlin, long before the term "digital nomad" entered the popular lexicon. Their efforts were often clumsy and fraught with challenges—unreliable connections, limited tools, and a world not yet equipped for their ambitions—but they proved a foundational concept: with a laptop and an internet connection, work was no longer shackled to a single desk.

The movement found its literary touchstone in 2007 with the publication of Timothy Ferriss's "The 4-Hour Workweek." The book was a cultural phenomenon, striking a chord with millions who felt trapped in the traditional work model. It wasn't just a guide to outsourcing and online business; it was a manifesto for a new philosophy of "lifestyle design." Ferriss evangelized the idea of creating systems that generated income with minimal active management, freeing up time and location to pursue one's passions. He gave a name and a methodology to the aspirations of a generation beginning to question the trade-offs of the conventional career path.

The book's central thesis—that time and mobility are the ultimate currencies—became a rallying cry. It legitimized the desire to escape the 9-to-5 and provided a practical, if ambitious, roadmap. While not everyone who read it managed to build a four-hour workweek, the book planted a powerful seed. It shifted the conversation from simply working remotely to strategically engineering a life of freedom and adventure. It inspired countless individuals to start online businesses, transition into freelancing, or negotiate remote work arrangements long before it was commonplace, forming the first major wave of modern digital nomads.

Of course, a cultural desire for change is inert without the tools to enact it. The true enabler of the digital nomad revolution has been the relentless, exponential march of technology. The slow, tethered internet of the early 2000s has given way to a global blanket of high-speed connectivity. The proliferation of Wi-Fi from a coffee shop luxury to a public utility, and the recent advent of 5G mobile networks, have made it possible to conduct high-stakes business from a remote island or a bustling foreign metropolis. This ubiquitous connectivity is the invisible infrastructure upon which the entire lifestyle is built.

Alongside connectivity, the rise of cloud computing was a critical development. Services like Dropbox, Google Drive, and iCloud effectively dematerialized the office file cabinet. Documents, projects, and entire archives were no longer confined to a single hard drive or a company server but became accessible from any device, anywhere in the world. This untethering of data was a monumental step, providing the security and flexibility necessary for a truly mobile professional life. It meant that the loss or failure of a laptop, while inconvenient, was no longer a catastrophic business-ending event.

Simultaneously, a new generation of collaboration tools emerged to dissolve the barriers of distance. The early days of clunky email chains and expensive international calls gave way to sophisticated platforms designed for seamless teamwork. Skype first normalized video calling, making face-to-face meetings possible across continents. Later, tools like Slack created virtual office environments, with channels for team chats, project updates, and casual water-cooler conversations. Project management software such as Asana, Trello, and Jira allowed teams to track progress and assign tasks with perfect clarity, regardless of their physical locations. This new digital toolkit effectively replicated, and in many cases improved upon, the collaborative functions of a traditional office.

The hardware itself also evolved. The heavy, underpowered laptops of the past have been replaced by ultralight, powerful devices with all-day battery life. The smartphone has become a pocket-sized command center, capable of handling everything from email and banking to video conferencing and content creation. The convergence of powerful, portable hardware and sophisticated, cloud-based software created the perfect technological ecosystem for location independence. The barrier to entry was no longer access to expensive corporate infrastructure, but simply the cost of a good laptop and a reliable internet plan.

Technology laid the foundation, but a profound cultural shift provided the motivation. For generations raised in the shadow of economic instability, from the dot-com bust to the 2008 financial crisis, the promise of a stable, lifelong job with a single company began to seem like an outdated fantasy. The social contract that had tied loyalty to security was broken. This led many, particularly millennials and Gen Z, to view their careers not as a linear ladder but as a "portfolio" of experiences, skills, and projects. The gig economy wasn't just a trend; it was a reflection of this new, more fluid approach to work.

This changing perspective on work coincided with a broader shift in consumer values, particularly the prioritization of experiences over material possessions. The new status symbol was no longer a luxury car or a larger house, but a passport full of stamps and a feed full of memories. This "experience economy" was fueled by a desire for personal growth, cultural immersion, and a life story worth telling. Travel, once seen as a brief escape from real life, was now viewed as an essential component of a life well-lived.

The travel industry itself was undergoing a parallel revolution that made the nomadic dream more attainable. The rise of budget airlines dramatically lowered the cost of international and regional flights, turning what was once a major expenditure into a manageable expense. Platforms like Airbnb, Booking.com, and Hostelworld democratized accommodation, offering a vast range of affordable alternatives to traditional hotels. These tools made it easy to find and book lodging for weeks or months at a time, providing the stability needed to live and work effectively in a new place. The friction and cost of long-term travel were being systematically erased.

Into this simmering pot of technological capability and cultural yearning, the COVID-19 pandemic dropped like a global catalyst. The sudden, forced transition to remote work for a significant portion of the global workforce was the largest workplace experiment in human history. Overnight, long-held corporate dogmas about the necessity of in-person collaboration and supervision were shattered. Companies that had resisted remote work for years were forced to adapt, and to their surprise, many found that productivity did not plummet. In some cases, it even increased.

This period acted as a proof of concept on a massive scale. It demonstrated to both employers and employees that effective, professional work could be accomplished from anywhere with a decent internet connection. The mystique and fear surrounding remote work evaporated, replaced by a widespread acceptance of its viability. The genie was out of the bottle. Millions of workers had a taste of a life without a daily commute, with more control over their schedules, and with greater autonomy in their daily lives.

The psychological impact of the pandemic was just as significant. The global crisis prompted a collective re-evaluation of priorities, a phenomenon often dubbed the "Great Resignation." Faced with unprecedented uncertainty, people began to question the fundamental assumptions of their lives. Was the relentless grind worth it? Was their job providing fulfillment, or just a paycheck? The desire for a better work-life balance, for more time with family, and for a life aligned with personal values became a dominant cultural narrative. The digital nomad lifestyle, once a niche pursuit, emerged as a tangible and attractive answer to these questions.

As the world slowly reopened, a new landscape of work began to take shape. Many companies, recognizing the demand for flexibility and the potential to attract top talent, embraced permanent remote or hybrid work policies. This was a game-changer. Suddenly, the path to location independence was no longer restricted to freelancers and entrepreneurs. A full-time employee with a stable salary at a major corporation could now, with their company's blessing, take their job on the road. This opened the floodgates, dramatically expanding the demographic of potential digital nomads.

This confluence of factors has led to a radical redefinition of two of the most fundamental concepts in our lives: work and travel. In the nomadic paradigm, "work" is entirely decoupled from geography. It is measured not by hours spent in a chair or by physical presence, but by output, results, and accountability. This fosters a more autonomous and trust-based relationship between workers and employers. It also necessitates a shift toward asynchronous communication, where collaboration happens across time zones without the need for everyone to be online simultaneously. This focus on results over "presenteeism" is a more efficient and empowering way to work.

Similarly, "travel" is transformed from a frantic, short-term activity into a slower, more immersive experience. The digital nomad is not a tourist in the traditional sense. Tourists visit; nomads inhabit. By staying in a location for weeks or months, they move beyond the superficial landmarks and begin to engage with the local culture on a deeper level. They shop at local markets, frequent neighborhood cafes, and build genuine relationships with residents. This "slow travel" fosters a more authentic and sustainable form of tourism, contributing to the local economy in a more meaningful way than a fleeting cruise ship passenger ever could.

The true revolution lies in the fusion of these two redefined concepts. The digital nomad lifestyle erases the hard line that once separated our working lives from our exploratory adventures. An afternoon break can be a walk through a centuries-old European city, a weekend can be spent hiking a volcano, and a lunch meeting can be followed by a surf session. This integration creates a holistic rhythm of life where personal growth and professional contribution are not competing interests but complementary pursuits. Work becomes the engine that powers the exploration, and the exploration provides the inspiration and perspective that enriches the work.

Recognizing the immense economic and cultural potential of this growing demographic, the world has started to adapt. Governments, once wary of the legal gray areas of remote work, are now actively courting location-independent professionals. Dozens of countries, from Estonia and Croatia to Barbados and the UAE, have launched "digital nomad visas." These programs provide a clear legal framework for foreigners to reside and work remotely within their borders for extended periods, simplifying a process that was once a bureaucratic nightmare. This official recognition signals a global acknowledgment that digital nomadism is a legitimate and lasting phenomenon.

An entire ecosystem of services and infrastructure has sprung up to support this mobile population. The handful of pioneering co-working spaces has exploded into a global industry, with brands like WeWork and a multitude of independent spaces offering reliable internet, professional amenities, and a built-in community in virtually every major city. The concept of "co-living" has also gained traction, providing flexible, community-oriented housing solutions that combine private living quarters with shared communal spaces, instantly combating the isolation that can accompany a life on the road. From specialized health insurance plans to global banking solutions, the marketplace is rapidly evolving to meet the unique needs of the global citizen. This growing infrastructure removes many of the logistical hurdles, making the lifestyle more accessible and sustainable than ever before.

CHAPTER TWO: Is This Lifestyle for You? A Realistic Self-Assessment

The pull is strong. Chapter One laid out the powerful forces—technological, cultural, and personal—that have made the digital nomad lifestyle more accessible than ever. The images it conjures are of ultimate freedom: a life designed on your own terms, rich with new cultures, flavors, and experiences. It's a compelling narrative, and for the right person, it is an achievable and deeply rewarding reality. But before you sell your couch, pack your bags, and book a one-way ticket to Bali, it's crucial to pause and engage in a rigorous, clear-eyed self-assessment. The question is not simply, "Can I do this?" but rather, "Should I do this?"

This lifestyle, for all its undeniable benefits, is not a universal solution to the dissatisfaction of a conventional life. It is not an escape from your problems, but rather a relocation of them, often to places where you don't speak the language or have a local support system. The freedom it offers is inextricably linked to a demand for radical self-reliance. This chapter is your mirror. Its purpose is not to deter you but to arm you with self-awareness. By honestly evaluating your personality, your professional habits, and your personal needs, you can make an informed decision and, if you choose to proceed, build a nomadic life that fits who you are, not who you see on social media.

Let's begin by addressing the elephant in the room: the Instagram-perfect image of digital nomadism. You've seen it a hundred times—a sleek laptop perfectly angled next to an artisanal coffee or a tropical cocktail, with a pristine beach and turquoise water in the background. It's a powerful marketing image, but as a blueprint for a workday, it is a comical failure. The reality involves squinting against the blinding sun glare on your screen, the persistent fear of a rogue wave splashing your expensive electronics, sand finding its way into every crevice of your keyboard, and the awkward dance of trying to find a power outlet.

The real work of a digital nomad happens in far less glamorous, though often equally interesting, settings. It happens in the quiet corner of a bustling city café, in the sterile, focused environment of a co-working space, or on the slightly-too-small desk in a short-term rental apartment. The adventure happens *around* the work, not necessarily *during* it. The first step in a realistic self-assessment is to mentally separate the work from the vacation. This is a work-centric lifestyle that facilitates travel, not a permanent holiday that occasionally involves checking emails. If the fantasy is your primary motivation, the reality of deadlines and deliverables in a foreign land can be a jarring wake-up call.

At the core of a successful nomadic life are certain personality traits that have less to do with your professional skills and more to do with your fundamental disposition. The most critical of these is self-discipline. In a traditional office environment, structure is imposed upon you. Your boss is down the hall, your colleagues are at the next desk, and the fixed hours of 9-to-5 create a clear boundary between work and leisure. As a digital nomad, that entire external structure vanishes. You are the CEO of your own productivity.

Ask yourself honestly: Are you a self-starter? When you have a project with a distant deadline, do you chip away at it consistently, or do you leave it all for a frantic, last-minute push? The temptations on the road are infinite. There will always be a new city to explore, an interesting person to meet, or a local festival to attend. Without the ability to say "no" to distractions and "yes" to buckling down and focusing, your work will suffer, your income will dry up, and the dream will quickly unravel. The freedom to create your own schedule is a double-edged sword; it requires the discipline to actually create one and, more importantly, to stick to it.

Hand in hand with discipline comes adaptability. A nomadic life is a life of constant, low-grade uncertainty. Your meticulously planned travel day can be upended by a canceled flight. The apartment you booked can look nothing like the pictures online. The Wi-Fi in your new city might be infuriatingly slow, right when you have a critical video call. These are not occasional inconveniences; they are regular features of the lifestyle. Your reaction to them will determine your sustainability as a nomad.

How do you typically respond when things go wrong? Do you become flustered, angry, and paralyzed by the disruption, or do you take a deep breath and start methodically looking for a solution? If you thrive on predictability, routine, and having every detail perfectly controlled, the inherent chaos of constant travel can be profoundly stressful. The successful nomad learns to embrace a certain level of flux. They become expert problem-solvers, adept at finding a Plan B, and then a Plan C. They view unexpected challenges not as disasters but as part of the adventure—a story to be told later.

This leads directly to the skill of resilience. You will face setbacks. You will make mistakes. You will have days where you question your sanity and your choices. You might get scammed, you might get sick in a country where you can't communicate effectively, or you might just have a project fall through at the worst possible moment. Resilience is the ability to bounce back from these experiences, to learn from them without letting them derail you. It's about understanding that a bad day, or even a bad week, in an amazing location is still just a bad day. It's the mental fortitude to keep going when the initial excitement wears off and the real work begins.

Finally, consider your relationship with material possessions. The digital nomad lifestyle is an exercise in practical minimalism. While you don't have to reduce your worldly belongings to a single 40-liter backpack, you must get comfortable with the idea of living with less. Every object you own is something you have to carry, pack, unpack, and worry about. Are you attached to your extensive library of physical books, your collection of kitchen gadgets, or a wardrobe for every conceivable social situation?

This isn't just a logistical consideration; it's a psychological one. For many, possessions are tied to a sense of identity, comfort, and home. The nomad must learn to find that sense of home within themselves, not in their external environment. They prioritize experiences over things, access over ownership. If the thought of paring down your belongings to what can fit in a suitcase or two fills you with genuine anxiety, it's an important feeling to examine. You may need to work through that attachment before you can fully embrace the lightness and freedom of a mobile life.

Beyond your internal disposition, it's vital to assess your social and emotional needs. Human beings are social creatures, and while technology allows us to stay connected, it is not a perfect substitute for in-person community. The single greatest challenge for many digital nomads, even the most introverted ones, is loneliness. The lifestyle is a series of hellos and goodbyes. You will meet incredible people and form fast, intense friendships, only to have to say farewell a few weeks or months later.

Be honest about your social constitution. Do you draw your energy primarily from a small, stable group of close friends and family? Or do you thrive on meeting new people and engaging in more transient, but still meaningful, social interactions? While you will build a global network over time, it takes effort to find your tribe in each new location. You must be comfortable with initiating conversations, putting yourself in new social situations like co-working events or local meetups, and being your own social director. You will spend a significant amount of time alone, and you need to be not just tolerant of your own company, but genuinely comfortable with it.

If you are considering this lifestyle with a partner or family, the complexity increases exponentially. It is no longer just your own assessment that matters, but a joint one. Does your partner share your enthusiasm for this lifestyle, or are they reluctantly coming along? How will you navigate disagreements in high-stress travel situations? For families with children, the considerations multiply to include schooling, socialization, and stability. While thousands of "nomad families" are thriving, it requires an exceptional level of communication, teamwork, and a shared commitment to the vision. The lifestyle can put immense pressure on relationships, and it's essential to ensure you are starting from a foundation of strength.

There is also the "fear of missing out" back home, or FOMO. While you are watching a beautiful sunset in Portugal, your friends back home are celebrating a wedding. While you are navigating a market in Vietnam, your family is gathering for a significant birthday. You cannot be in two places at once. The nomadic life is a trade-off. You gain a world of new experiences, but you inevitably miss out on important moments with your established community. Consider how you will feel seeing those events unfold on social media from thousands of miles away. A certain level of acceptance and a proactive effort to stay connected are necessary to manage these feelings.

Next, turn the lens on your professional life. Not all remote jobs are created equal, and not all work styles are suited for this path. First, consider your ideal work environment. Do you feed off the creative energy of a bustling office and enjoy spontaneous brainstorming sessions with colleagues? If so, the isolation of working alone in an apartment could be a shock to your system. While co-working spaces can mitigate this, they don't fully replicate the dynamic of a consistent team in a shared space. Conversely, if you are a "deep worker" who requires long, uninterrupted stretches of silence to be productive, you might find this lifestyle a perfect fit.

You must also evaluate the specifics of your job. Does it require you to be online during specific hours that align with a particular time zone? A marketing manager in Bangkok who needs to be on 9 AM New York time calls is signing up for a nocturnal work life, which can be draining and unsustainable. The most flexible jobs for nomads are often asynchronous, meaning the work is project-based and communication does not need to happen in real-time. This allows you to adapt your work hours to your location and energy levels.

Then there is the financial reality. We will dive deep into budgeting and financial planning in Chapter Eight, but for this initial assessment, the questions are more fundamental. What is your tolerance for financial uncertainty? If you are a freelancer, your income may be variable. Can you handle the stress of a month where you land no new clients? Do you have a sufficient savings buffer—typically three to six months of expenses—to act as a safety net? The "broke backpacker" trope does not mix well with the professional demands of being a digital nomad. Financial stress is a primary reason why many aspiring nomads burn out and go home. You need a solid financial footing before you even start.

Consider your long-term career ambitions. The digital nomad path can be fantastic for skill acquisition and building a diverse portfolio, but it can make a traditional corporate climb more difficult. Opportunities for mentorship, management experience, and internal promotions can be harder to come by when you are not physically present in a central office. This is not to say that career growth is impossible—many nomads build incredibly successful businesses and careers—but the trajectory is often less linear. You must be comfortable with forging your own path and defining success on your own terms, which may look different from your peers back home.

Finally, do not neglect your physical and mental health. A stable routine is often the bedrock of well-being, and the nomadic lifestyle is inherently disruptive to routine. How will you maintain your fitness regimen when you are constantly changing gyms or running routes? If you require regular medication or therapy, how will you manage that across different countries with varying healthcare systems? It is imperative to have a proactive plan for managing your health on the road. For your mental health, be aware that the constant change, potential loneliness, and stress of navigating new environments can be taxing. Having established coping mechanisms, whether it's meditation, journaling, or regular video calls with a therapist, is not a luxury but a necessity.

After considering these facets of your life—personality, social needs, professional realities, and health—you may still be unsure. The good news is that this is not an all-or-nothing proposition. You do not have to sell everything you own to find out if this life is for you. The smartest approach is to arrange a "test drive." Take a "workcation" for two or three weeks. Go to a new city, but keep your regular work hours. Don't treat it like a vacation. Find a co-working space, do your grocery shopping, and simulate the actual day-to-day life.

An even better test is to try a one-to-three-month stint in a single location. This gives you enough time to get past the initial tourist phase and experience the realities of setting up a temporary life. You'll have to find a routine, deal with local bureaucracy, and perhaps even experience the first pangs of loneliness or homesickness. This trial period provides invaluable data. You might discover that you love it even more than you imagined. Or, you might find that you prefer the stability of a home base, and there is absolutely no shame in that. The goal is self-discovery, not a forced outcome.

This chapter of self-reflection is arguably the most important work you will do before you ever pack a bag. It is the process of building a solid foundation of self-awareness. Being a successful and, more importantly, a happy digital nomad is not about being a certain type of person. There are introverted and extroverted nomads, hyper-organized and go-with-the-flow nomads, nomads in their twenties and nomads in their seventies. Success lies in understanding your own nature—your strengths, weaknesses, and non-negotiables—and then consciously designing a nomadic life that honors them. It is about knowing yourself well enough to build the right support systems to thrive anywhere in the world.

CHAPTER THREE: The Mindset for Success: Embracing Flexibility and Resilience

You have looked in the mirror. The self-assessment in the previous chapter was the critical first step, a candid inventory of your natural inclinations, your social needs, and your professional realities. It may have filled you with confidence, or it may have revealed areas that give you pause. Regardless of the outcome, the most important takeaway is this: the traits that define a successful digital nomad are not set in stone. They are not personality quirks you either have or you don't. They are muscles. The mindset for thriving on the road is a skill to be learned, a discipline to be practiced, and a mentality to be cultivated. This is where the real work begins—not in an airport, but in your own head.

Success in this lifestyle is less about the perfection of your planning and more about the quality of your response when those plans inevitably go awry. It's about building an internal framework that can withstand the constant flux of a life in motion. This chapter is your psychological toolkit. We will move beyond identifying the necessary traits and focus on the daily practices and mental shifts required to develop them. Forget the fantasy of a flawless journey; instead, let's focus on building the grit and grace to navigate the beautiful, messy, and unpredictable reality.

The first and most foundational pillar of the nomadic mindset is flexibility. This is a word that gets thrown around casually, often mistaken for a simple, go-with-the-flow passivity. True flexibility, however, is an active and strategic practice. It is not the absence of a plan, but the refusal to be emotionally derailed when the plan changes. It is the art of holding your goals loosely while holding your resolve tightly. The seasoned nomad understands that Plan A is often just a pleasant suggestion, a starting point from which the real adventure begins.

Imagine you have just landed in Lisbon, with a month-long apartment rental secured and plans to explore the city's vibrant neighborhoods. On day three, you receive an email: a sudden plumbing issue means you have to vacate the apartment in 48 hours. The passive traveler panics. They see their meticulously laid plans crumbling, and the stress of finding a new place on short notice eclipses any potential enjoyment. The flexible nomad, while certainly annoyed, sees a different set of possibilities. Their mind immediately pivots. Could this be an opportunity to explore a different city, like Porto, for a couple of weeks? Is there a co-living space they were curious about that might have last-minute availability? The disruption is reframed from a crisis into an unexpected detour, a new chapter in the story.

This mental pivot is not an accident; it is a trained response. It comes from the practice of pre-emptively creating a Plan B and a Plan C for every major decision. When you book a flight, you mentally acknowledge the possibility of a cancellation and know what your alternative routes would be. When you rely on a single client for the bulk of your income, you are already thinking about how to diversify your client base. This "what if" thinking is not a form of pessimism; it is a form of strategic empowerment. It strips unexpected events of their power to induce panic, transforming you from a victim of circumstance into an agile problem-solver.

If flexibility is the shock absorber that smooths out the bumps in the road, resilience is the engine that keeps you moving forward after a genuine breakdown. Life on the road will, at some point, present you with challenges that go beyond mere inconvenience. You may have your laptop stolen, experience a significant health issue, or face a major professional setback. These are the moments that test your resolve and tempt you to book a one-way ticket home. Resilience is the mental fortitude that allows you to absorb these blows, process them, and continue the journey, not just in spite of them, but often strengthened by them.

Like a muscle, resilience is built through progressive resistance. You don't start by lifting the heaviest weight in the gym. Similarly, you build resilience by navigating smaller, everyday challenges. It starts with the minor frustrations: the train that is thirty minutes late, the restaurant that gets your order wrong, the Wi-Fi that cuts out mid-call. In these moments, you have a choice. You can let frustration and anger consume you, or you can take a deep breath and practice acceptance. Each time you choose the latter, you are performing a single "rep" in your resilience training.

A powerful technique for building resilience is active reframing. When faced with a setback, consciously work to change the narrative you tell yourself about it. The freelance project that was suddenly cancelled isn't a disaster that proves your incompetence; it is an unexpected block of free time to upskill, network, or work on your own passion project. Getting lost in a new city isn't a sign of your poor navigational skills; it is an opportunity to discover a hidden gem of a neighborhood you would have otherwise missed. It's about learning to see the opportunity within the obstacle. This isn't about toxic positivity or ignoring genuine difficulties; it's about shifting your focus from what you've lost to what you might gain.

Underpinning both flexibility and resilience is the psychological concept of a "growth mindset," a term popularized by psychologist Carol Dweck. Individuals with a fixed mindset believe that their intelligence, talents, and abilities are static, unchangeable traits. When faced with a challenge, their primary goal is to avoid failure and appearing incompetent. In contrast, those with a growth mindset believe that their abilities can be developed through dedication and hard work. They see challenges not as threats, but as opportunities to learn and grow. For a digital nomad, cultivating a growth mindset is not optional; it is essential for survival.

Every day on the road presents you with situations where a fixed mindset would lead to paralysis. Trying to decipher a public transport map in a language you don't understand, navigating a complex visa application process, or learning how to use a new piece of project management software are all potential triggers. The fixed mindset says, "I'm not good with languages," or "I'm terrible with bureaucracy." It shuts down the problem-solving process before it can even begin.

The growth mindset, however, adds a single, powerful word to those sentences: "yet." "I'm not good with languages *yet*." "I haven't figured out this visa process *yet*." This simple addition transforms a statement of permanent limitation into a statement of a temporary state. It opens the door to curiosity and action. It encourages you to download a translation app, to ask a local for help, to break down the visa application into smaller, manageable steps. Adopting this mindset means you view every new country, every new challenge, and every mistake as part of your global curriculum.

This leads directly to the practice of developing a problem-solving orientation. A core tenet of the successful nomad is the belief that everything is, in some way, "figure-out-able." This doesn't mean that every problem has a simple solution, but that every problem has a next step. When confronted with an issue—say, your bank has frozen your account due to suspicious foreign activity—the key is to resist the urge to feel helpless. Instead, you immediately shift into action-oriented brainstorming. What is the first, most logical step? Find the bank's international helpline. What if that doesn't work? Can you contact them through a secure online portal? Is there a time when it would be better to call, considering time zones? Who do you know who might have faced a similar issue?

This transforms you from a passive recipient of problems into an active agent of solutions. It is a mindset that thrives on resourcefulness. You become an expert at using the tools at your disposal: Google searches, online forums, expatriate groups on social media, translation apps, and, most importantly, the kindness of strangers. You learn to approach challenges with a sense of playful curiosity, almost like a puzzle to be solved. This orientation is a profound source of empowerment, proving to yourself again and again that you are capable of handling whatever the world throws at you.

Of course, not all problems can be solved through sheer force of will. A significant part of the nomadic mindset is learning the subtle art of letting go. You must develop a profound sense of patience and accept that you cannot control the world around you. You cannot control the speed of the immigration line, the schedule of the local bus service, or the fact that many businesses in Spain close for several hours in the middle of the day. Attempting to impose your own cultural expectations of efficiency and timeliness onto a different culture is a surefire recipe for chronic frustration.

Radical acceptance is the practice of acknowledging reality without resisting it. The bus is late. This is a fact. Wasting your energy on anger and frustration will not make it arrive any sooner. Instead, you can accept the reality of the situation and choose how to use that unexpected pocket of time. Can you answer a few emails on your phone? Can you practice your language skills with a vocabulary app? Or can you simply sit, observe the world around you, and enjoy a moment of unplanned stillness? This practice of letting go of control reduces stress and opens you up to the actual experience of where you are, rather than the experience you think you *should* be having.

The most effective antidote to the frustration that arises from cultural differences is a cultivated sense of curiosity. When you encounter a custom that seems illogical, inefficient, or just plain strange, your default reaction might be judgment. The curious nomad learns to consciously override this impulse and replace it with a question: "Why?" Why do people in this country slurp their noodles so loudly? Why is it considered polite to be fifteen minutes late for a social engagement here? Approaching these differences with genuine curiosity transforms a potential point of conflict into a rich learning opportunity.

This open-mindedness extends beyond simple customs to the very fabric of how you see the world. Immersing yourself in different cultures will inevitably challenge your own deeply held beliefs and assumptions. It forces you to recognize that the way you were raised to do things is just one way among thousands. This can be a destabilizing experience, but it is also an incredibly enriching one. An open and curious mind allows you to collect new perspectives, to learn from different ways of living and working, and to ultimately become a more empathetic and well-rounded human being.

Finally, and perhaps most importantly, the successful nomadic mindset is one that is rooted in self-compassion. This journey is difficult. There will be days when you feel profoundly lonely, homesick, and overwhelmed. There will be times when you make a costly mistake, miss a deadline, or feel like you are failing at both work and travel. In these moments, your internal monologue is critical. A harsh, self-critical voice will only spiral you further into despair.

Self-compassion is the practice of treating yourself with the same kindness and understanding you would offer a good friend. It is acknowledging that it is okay to have a bad day. It is giving yourself permission to spend an entire Saturday binge-watching a familiar show on Netflix instead of forcing yourself to go sightseeing. It is recognizing when you are approaching burnout and proactively scheduling a "vacation from your travel" — a week of staying in one place, eating familiar food, and simply resting. You must learn to be your own greatest ally on this journey. Without self-compassion, the relentless demands of work, travel, and self-reliance can lead to a swift and brutal burnout.

These components—flexibility, resilience, a growth mindset, a problem-solving orientation, the ability to let go, curiosity, and self-compassion—are not separate attributes. They are interconnected elements of a single, powerful mindset. They reinforce one another, creating a virtuous cycle. A growth mindset makes you more resilient. Curiosity makes you more flexible. Self-compassion gives you the strength to keep practicing all of them. Building this internal foundation is the most important preparation you can undertake. It is the invisible luggage that will carry you through every challenge and allow you to fully embrace the unparalleled freedom this lifestyle has to offer.

CHAPTER FOUR: Choosing Your Path: Freelancing, Remote Employment, and Entrepreneurship

The mindset is in place, the self-assessment is complete. You understand the internal resilience required for a life of motion. Now we arrive at the engine that powers the entire journey: your income. The romantic vision of the digital nomad life, full of freedom and exploration, is sustained by the decidedly unromantic reality of consistent cash flow. Without a reliable way to fund your travels, your grand adventure becomes a short, stressful, and ultimately unsustainable holiday. The question of *how* you will earn money is not just a logistical detail; it is the central pillar upon which your new life will be built.

Fortunately, the digital economy has opened up multiple avenues for the location-independent professional. These paths are not created equal. They vary wildly in their levels of autonomy, stability, risk, and reward. There is no single "best" choice, only the choice that best aligns with your skills, your financial situation, your risk tolerance, and the lifestyle you ultimately want to lead. This chapter will dissect the three primary models: freelancing, the path of the self-employed specialist; remote employment, the route of the location-independent employee; and entrepreneurship, the high-stakes game of the business builder. Understanding the distinct DNA of each is the first step in crafting a career that doesn't just allow you to travel, but empowers you to thrive.

The Original Nomad's Route: Freelancing

Freelancing is the quintessential digital nomad path, the model that powered the first wave of location-independent pioneers. At its core, a freelancer is a self-employed professional who offers specialized services to multiple clients on a contract or project basis. You are, in essence, a business of one. You are not selling a product, but your time, your expertise, and your skill. The roster of freelance professions is vast and ever-expanding, including writers, graphic designers, web developers, marketing consultants, virtual assistants, translators, and project managers. If a skill can be delivered digitally, it can be freelanced.

The greatest allure of freelancing is autonomy. As a freelancer, you are the master of your own professional destiny. You choose the clients you work with, the projects you take on, and, crucially, the rates you charge. There is no boss dictating your hours or your workload. If you want to work intensely for four days and take a three-day weekend to hike a volcano, you can. If you want to take the entire month of October off to explore a new country, you can—provided you have managed your finances and client expectations accordingly. This level of control over your schedule is the ultimate expression of the freedom that draws so many to the nomadic life.

This autonomy also extends to your earning potential. Unlike a salaried employee, your income is not capped. Your earnings are a direct result of your effort and your value in the marketplace. As your skills sharpen and your reputation grows, you can command higher rates. You can choose to work more hours to fund a specific goal or work fewer hours to enjoy more leisure time. This direct correlation between work and reward can be incredibly motivating, offering a clear path to increasing your income based on merit and hustle. Furthermore, working with a diverse array of clients on varied projects is a powerful catalyst for skill development, exposing you to new industries and challenges that keep your professional life engaging and your resume robust.

However, this freedom comes at a price. The flip side of "ultimate autonomy" is "total responsibility." The most significant challenge for most freelancers is income instability. The work landscape can be a roller coaster of "feast or famine." You may find yourself juggling multiple lucrative projects one month, only to face a dry pipeline the next. This requires a level of financial discipline that is not optional. Building a substantial cash buffer (a minimum of three to six months of living expenses) is not just a good idea; it is a prerequisite for survival. Without it, the stress of a slow month can quickly erode the joy of the lifestyle.

Moreover, a freelancer wears many hats. You are not just the writer or the developer; you are also the chief marketing officer, the head of sales, the bookkeeper, and the customer service representative. A significant portion of your time will be spent not on your core craft, but on the administrative tasks of running a business: prospecting for new clients, writing proposals, sending invoices, and chasing late payments. This "hustle" is perpetual. Your work is never truly done, because you must always have one eye on the next project. For those who simply want to do the work they love, the constant demand for self-promotion and business development can be exhausting.

Finally, you are on your own. There is no corporate safety net. Health insurance, retirement contributions, paid vacation, and sick days are entirely on you to fund and manage. This adds a layer of complexity and cost that salaried employees don't have to consider. The isolation can also be a challenge. You lack the built-in camaraderie of a team and the professional guidance of a manager. Success requires a high degree of self-motivation and the proactive effort to build your own professional network. This path is best suited for the disciplined self-starter, the individual who has a marketable skill and is comfortable with the risks and responsibilities of being their own boss.

The Stability Seeker's Choice: Remote Employment

The rise of mainstream remote work has opened up a powerful alternative to the freelance grind. As a remote employee, you are a full- or part-time employee of a single company. The structure is familiar: you have a job title, a manager, a team of colleagues, and a defined set of responsibilities. The revolutionary difference is that your job is not tied to a specific office. Your employer gives you the flexibility to perform your duties from a location of your choosing, whether that's a home office, a co-working space in Tulum, or a café in Taipei.

The single greatest advantage of this model is stability. A remote job provides a predictable, recurring paycheck. This consistency removes the primary stressor of freelance life and makes financial planning exponentially easier. You know exactly how much money is coming in each month, allowing you to budget for your travel, accommodation, and savings with confidence. This financial security provides a solid foundation that can make the nomadic lifestyle feel far more manageable and less precarious, especially for those just starting out.

Beyond the steady income, remote employment often comes with a package of benefits that freelancers can only dream of. Company-sponsored health insurance, contributions to a retirement plan, and, perhaps most importantly, paid time off are standard in many remote roles. This not only represents a significant financial savings but also removes a massive administrative burden. Knowing you have paid vacation days allows you to fully disconnect and enjoy your travels without worrying about a loss of income. Sick leave means you can recover from an illness without the added stress of missing a project deadline.

Being part of a company also provides a built-in structure and community. You have colleagues to collaborate with, a manager to provide guidance and feedback, and a shared corporate mission. This can be a powerful antidote to the isolation that many nomads experience. Virtual team meetings, Slack channels, and company retreats (often held in exciting locations) can foster a strong sense of belonging and camaraderie. Furthermore, remote employment can offer a more defined career path, with opportunities for mentorship, promotions, and professional development that may be less clear in the freelance world.

This stability, however, comes with a trade-off in autonomy. While you have the freedom of location, you are still an employee. You do not get to choose your projects, your clients, or your boss. Your work is dictated by the needs and priorities of the company. The most significant constraint is often time. Many remote jobs are not fully asynchronous and require you to be online and available during specific business hours, typically tied to the time zone of the company's headquarters. This can severely limit your travel options. A job that requires you to work 9 AM to 5 PM Eastern Standard Time is manageable from Latin America but becomes a nocturnal nightmare if you're trying to live in Southeast Asia.

You must also operate within the confines of company policy. Your "work from anywhere" dream might collide with the legal and logistical reality of your employer. Some companies may have restrictions on which countries you can work from due to tax implications, data security laws, or other legal complexities. Before you take a remote job with nomadic aspirations, it is crucial to have a transparent conversation with your employer about their specific policies regarding international work. The golden handcuffs can be comfortable, but they are still handcuffs. Remote employment is an excellent path for those who value security and structure, enjoy being part of a team, and are willing to trade some autonomy for a great deal of stability.

The Empire Builder's Gamble: Entrepreneurship

The third path is the most demanding, the most difficult, and potentially the most rewarding: entrepreneurship. This goes a step beyond freelancing. As an entrepreneur, you are not just selling your own time; you are building a scalable system or asset that can generate income independently of your direct, hour-by-hour involvement. This is the realm of creating a software-as-a-service (SaaS) product, building an e-commerce brand, developing and selling online courses, or creating a content-based business (like a monetized blog, podcast, or YouTube channel) with a large audience.

The ultimate promise of entrepreneurship is scalability. A freelancer can only earn as much as the hours they can work and the rate they can charge. An employee's salary has a defined ceiling. A successful business, however, has theoretically unlimited growth potential. You are creating something that can serve hundreds, thousands, or even millions of customers at once.

This is the path that leads to passive income—money that is earned without you actively trading your time for it. A well-designed online course can be sold to students while you sleep. A popular e-commerce store can process orders while you are on a plane. This decoupling of time and income is the holy grail for many nomads.

Being an entrepreneur offers the highest degree of creative and strategic freedom. You are building your vision from the ground up. Every decision—from the product's design to the marketing strategy to the company's culture—is yours to make. This can be an incredibly fulfilling pursuit for those who are driven by a desire to create and innovate. A successful business is also a valuable asset. Unlike a freelance reputation or a job, which vanishes when you stop working, a business can be sold, providing a significant financial exit that can fund your goals for years to come.

This immense potential comes with an equally immense level of risk and pressure. The journey of an entrepreneur is often front-loaded with a staggering amount of work for little to no initial pay. It may require a significant investment of your own savings to get the business off the ground. While a freelancer starts earning with their first client, an entrepreneur might work for months or even years before their venture becomes profitable, if it ever does. The failure rate for new businesses is notoriously high, and you must have the financial runway and the emotional resilience to weather this uncertain and often stressful initial phase.

The responsibility can be all-consuming. The romantic notion of the entrepreneur sipping cocktails on the beach while their business runs itself is a myth, at least for the first several years. In reality, the entrepreneur often works longer and harder than both the freelancer and the employee. You are responsible for everything. When a server crashes at 3 AM, you are the one who has to fix it. When a customer has a major complaint, the buck stops with you. This weight of responsibility can make it difficult to disconnect and can, ironically, leave you with less time and mental energy to enjoy your travels than the other two paths.

Entrepreneurship is a high-stakes gamble. It is a path for the visionary, the system-builder, and the individual with an unshakeable belief in their idea and a profound tolerance for risk. It requires a long-term perspective and the grit to push through constant challenges and setbacks. It is not a quick route to a laptop lifestyle, but rather a demanding and all-encompassing quest to build something of lasting value.

It is also important to recognize that these paths are not rigid, mutually exclusive silos. They exist on a spectrum, and many successful nomads create a hybrid model that suits their needs. A remote employee might take on freelance projects on the side to earn extra income and explore new skills. A successful freelancer, tired of trading time for money, might begin to "productize" their services by creating an online course, taking their first steps into entrepreneurship. An early-stage entrepreneur might do some freelance consulting to bootstrap their business and keep the lights on. Your path can, and likely will, evolve. The key is to start with a clear-eyed understanding of each option, choosing the one that provides the right balance of freedom and security for you, right now.

CHAPTER FIVE: In-Demand Skills for the Modern Nomad: Crafting Your Remote Career

You've chosen your path—or at least have a clearer picture of the risks and rewards of freelancing, remote employment, and entrepreneurship. That decision provides the vehicle for your journey. Now, you need to fuel it. The engine of a sustainable nomadic life is a marketable, location-independent skill. While the desire for freedom is universal, the ability to fund that freedom is built upon a specific set of professional competencies that can be delivered through a Wi-Fi connection. Not all careers are created equal in their adaptability to a life on the move. A surgeon or a master carpenter cannot simply pack up their trade and practice from a café in Chiang Mai.

The modern nomad's career is built on a foundation of digital delivery. The work product—be it code, a design file, a marketing report, or a well-crafted article—can be sent across the globe in an instant. This chapter is a practical survey of the professional landscape, designed to help you identify where your existing talents might fit or, alternatively, to illuminate the most promising skills to acquire. We will explore the concrete, in-demand professions that are powering the remote work revolution, moving from the abstract desire to "work online" to the tangible reality of a viable remote career. This isn't about finding a temporary gig; it's about building a professional identity that is as mobile as you are.

Before diving into specific job titles, it is crucial to recognize a set of universal skills that form the bedrock of any successful remote career. These are the meta-skills, the professional habits that enable you to perform any digital job effectively from anywhere in the world. The most important of these is exceptional written communication. In a remote setting, the casual hallway conversation or the quick pop-by-a-desk question is gone. The vast majority of your interactions with clients and colleagues will happen through text—on platforms like Slack, in emails, and in project management software. Your ability to convey complex ideas, ask precise questions, and provide clear, concise updates without the benefit of tone or body language is paramount. Ambiguity is the enemy of remote work, and clarity in writing is your greatest weapon against it.

Coupled with communication is an almost fanatical level of self-management. As we explored in the mindset chapter, the external structures of an office are absent. This means you must become a master of your own time and energy. It's not just about avoiding the temptation of a midday siesta; it's about proactively structuring your workday, setting realistic deadlines for yourself, and tracking your own progress without a manager looking over your shoulder. Tools like Asana, Trello, or even a simple, well-organized to-do list become your personal supervisors. The ability to break down large projects into manageable tasks and execute them consistently is what separates the thriving nomad from the one who is constantly behind schedule.

Finally, a proactive problem-solving attitude is non-negotiable. When you are in a different time zone from your team or client, you cannot always wait for an immediate answer to a question. The most valuable remote professionals are those who, upon hitting a roadblock, don't just stop and wait for instructions. They anticipate potential issues, research possible solutions independently, and present their findings along with the problem. This "here's the issue, and here are three ways I think we can solve it" approach demonstrates initiative and makes you an invaluable, low-friction member of any team. These soft skills are the operating system upon which all the following technical skills run.

The Technical Toolkit: Careers in Code and Development

The world runs on software, making technical skills some of the most durable and in-demand in the remote marketplace. If you have a logical mind and enjoy building things, a career in development offers a clear and often lucrative path to location independence. The work is almost entirely digital, project-based, and can often be done asynchronously, making it a perfect fit for the nomadic lifestyle.

Web Development is perhaps the most common entry point. It's broadly divided into three areas. Front-End Developers are the architects of the user experience; they use languages like HTML, CSS, and JavaScript to build the visible parts of a website that a user interacts with. They focus on making the site look good and function smoothly. Back-End Developers work behind the scenes, building and maintaining the server, application, and database that power the front end. They use languages like Python, Ruby, Java, or PHP to handle things like user accounts and data processing. Full-Stack Developers are the versatile generalists who are proficient in both front-end and back-end technologies. The barrier to entry has lowered significantly, with countless high-quality online bootcamps and courses available to teach these skills from scratch.

Mobile App Development is another booming field. With billions of smartphone users worldwide, the demand for skilled iOS and Android developers continues to grow. These professionals use languages like Swift or Objective-C for Apple's iOS platform and Kotlin or Java for Google's Android. The work involves designing, building, and deploying applications that we use every day, from banking apps to games. Like web development, it is highly project-oriented and lends itself well to freelance contracts or full-time remote employment with tech companies of all sizes.

Beyond these more common paths lie a host of specialized and increasingly remote-friendly technical roles. Cybersecurity professionals work to protect computer systems and networks from theft or damage, a critical need for any company with an online presence. DevOps Engineers work to streamline the software development and deployment process, helping teams build and release software faster and more reliably. These fields often require more specialized training and experience but can offer higher pay and significant job security. The common thread is that the work is based on logic and code, deliverables are digital, and performance is measured by results, not by time spent in a chair.

The Creative Canvas: Design, Content, and Media

If your talents lean more towards the aesthetic than the algorithmic, the creative industries offer a wealth of opportunity for digital nomads. The rise of digital marketing and online media has created a voracious demand for high-quality visual and written content, and this work can be done from anywhere with a good laptop and a keen eye.

Graphic Design is a foundational creative skill for the digital age. From logos and branding packages for new businesses to social media graphics, website layouts, and marketing materials, the need for compelling visual communication is endless. Professionals in this space are masters of tools like Adobe Photoshop, Illustrator, and InDesign. A strong portfolio showcasing your design style and versatility is often more important than a formal degree, making it an accessible field for self-taught, talented individuals.

Building on this is the highly sought-after field of UI/UX Design. UI (User Interface) design is the visual part of the equation, focused on the look and feel of a product's interface—the buttons, menus, and typography. UX (User Experience) design is a broader discipline focused on the overall experience a person has when using a product. It involves research, user interviews, and wireframing to ensure that a website or app is not just beautiful, but also intuitive, efficient, and enjoyable to use. Tools like Figma and Sketch are the industry standards. The demand for skilled UI/UX designers has exploded as companies realize that a great user experience is a key competitive advantage.

Content Creation is a broad category that encompasses a range of disciplines. Writing is perhaps the most portable skill imaginable. Copywriters craft persuasive text for advertisements, websites, and emails, focusing on driving a specific action, like a purchase. Content Writers create informative or entertaining articles, blog posts, and guides designed to engage an audience and build a brand's authority. The ability to write clearly, adapt to different tones of voice, and understand the basics of search engine optimization (SEO) makes a writer a valuable asset to any business with an online presence.

Video Editing and Motion Graphics are also increasingly viable remote careers. As video becomes the dominant form of online content, the need for skilled editors who can turn raw footage into a polished final product has skyrocketed. Using software like Adobe Premiere Pro and Final Cut Pro, editors can work with clients from anywhere in the world, receiving footage via cloud services and delivering the finished product digitally. This field requires a more powerful laptop and faster internet for uploading and downloading large files, but it offers a dynamic and creative career path.

The Growth Engine: Marketing and Sales in the Digital Age

A great product or service is useless if no one knows it exists. This is where the marketing and sales professionals come in. These roles are focused on a company's growth, and in the digital era, the vast majority of this work is location-independent. The field is data-driven, strategic, and constantly evolving, offering a dynamic environment for the lifelong learner.

Digital Marketing is an umbrella term for a wide range of specialties. Search Engine Optimization (SEO) specialists work to improve a website's visibility on search engines like Google, a fundamental need for almost any business. Paid Advertising or Search Engine Marketing (SEM) managers create and manage campaigns on platforms like Google Ads and Facebook Ads, requiring an analytical mind and a knack for optimization. Social Media Managers develop and execute strategies to grow and engage a community on platforms like Instagram, TikTok, and LinkedIn. Each of these roles is highly measurable, making it easy to demonstrate your value to clients or employers regardless of your physical location.

Content Marketing is the strategic intersection of writing and marketing. Professionals in this field plan, create, and distribute valuable content to attract and retain a clearly defined audience. This goes beyond simply writing blog posts; it involves creating a comprehensive strategy that might include videos, podcasts, and ebooks, all designed to build trust and authority for a brand. It's a role that requires a blend of creativity and analytical skill, as success is measured by metrics like traffic, engagement, and lead generation.

Even the traditionally office-based field of Sales has moved online. Remote sales roles, often called Sales Development Representatives (SDRs) or Account Executives, are becoming increasingly common. These professionals use email, social media, and video calls to find, nurture, and close deals with new clients. While some roles may require alignment with a specific time zone for making calls, many B2B (business-to-business) sales cycles are managed effectively across continents. Strong communication skills and a resilient personality are key to success in this high-energy field.

The Organizational Backbone: Support and Operations

Not every remote role involves coding or creative design. A huge and often overlooked segment of the remote job market is dedicated to the operational tasks that keep businesses running smoothly. These roles are perfect for individuals who are highly organized, reliable, and excel at communication and coordination.

Virtual Assistant (VA) is one of the most popular and flexible entry points into the digital nomad world. VAs provide administrative, technical, or creative assistance to clients remotely. The tasks can be incredibly varied, from managing email inboxes and scheduling appointments to bookkeeping, social media posting, and customer service. The beauty of this role is its adaptability; you can start by offering a broad range of services and then specialize over time as you identify the tasks you are best at and enjoy the most.

43

Project Management is a more specialized operational role. As more companies adopt remote or distributed team structures, the need for skilled project managers who can keep complex projects on track and on budget has grown significantly. These individuals are the central hub of communication, using tools like Jira, Asana, or Monday.com to assign tasks, monitor progress, and ensure that deadlines are met. It requires excellent organizational skills, the ability to communicate effectively with diverse stakeholders, and a knack for staying calm under pressure.

Customer Support is the frontline of any business, and today, that frontline is overwhelmingly digital. Customer support representatives assist customers via email, live chat, and sometimes phone, answering questions and resolving issues. While some positions require you to be online during specific hours, many companies offer more flexible, 24/7 support structures that allow for more freedom. This role is ideal for those who are patient, empathetic, and genuinely enjoy helping people.

As you gain experience, you might evolve into a role like an Online Business Manager (OBM). An OBM is a step above a VA, taking a more strategic role in managing the day-to-day operations of an online business. They might oversee projects, manage a team of VAs, and work directly with the business owner to implement new systems and strategies. It's a leadership role that offers a great deal of responsibility and impact within a remote company.

The key to crafting your remote career is to find the intersection of three things: what you are good at, what you enjoy doing, and what the market is willing to pay for. Don't be afraid to start where you are. You can leverage skills from a previous office job and re-package them for a remote context. A former office manager has all the foundational skills to be an excellent virtual assistant. A traditional marketing professional can upskill on the latest digital tools. The path is not always about starting from zero; it is often about a strategic pivot. By focusing on developing a skill that is in high demand and can be delivered digitally, you are not just finding a job; you are building a key to a world of freedom and flexibility.

CHAPTER SIX: Landing Remote Work: Strategies for Finding the Best Opportunities

You have the right mindset, and you have a skill that can be delivered from anywhere with an internet connection. The foundation is solid, but a foundation alone doesn't pay for a flight to Florence or a month-long stay in Mexico City. Now comes the active part: the hunt. Landing your first, or your next, remote role is a job in itself. It requires a different approach than a traditional, location-based search. The pool of competition is global, but so is the pool of opportunity. The key is to move beyond passively scrolling through endless job postings and adopt a proactive, multi-channel strategy.

Think of your job search not as casting a single, large net, but as setting out multiple, specialized fishing lines in different parts of the digital ocean. Some will yield quick bites, others will require patience, and some will attract the big catch you weren't expecting. Relying on a single method is a recipe for frustration. A successful remote job search is a blend of actively pursuing advertised openings, cultivating your personal network, and positioning yourself so that opportunities begin to find you. This chapter is your guide to navigating these waters, from the bustling public marketplaces to the quiet, hidden coves where the best roles are often found.

The Digital Town Square: Remote Job Boards and Freelance Marketplaces

For most people starting their search, the first stop is an online job board. These websites are the central hubs of the remote work economy, aggregating thousands of opportunities from companies around the world. They are an excellent starting point for understanding what kinds of roles are available and which companies are hiring. However, it is crucial to know where to look, as not all job boards are created equal.

The most valuable are the curated, remote-first job boards. These platforms specialize exclusively in location-independent positions, which saves you the hassle of filtering through traditional listings that might have a vague "remote-friendly" tag. Sites like We Work Remotely, Remote.co, and Dynamite Jobs are pillars of the remote community, often featuring high-quality listings from established remote companies. Others, like FlexJobs, offer a wider range of flexible work, including remote, hybrid, and part-time roles, but require a subscription fee, which can help to weed out some of the competition. These sites are your primary hunting grounds for full-time remote employment.

For freelancers, the equivalent is the online marketplace. Platforms like Upwork and Fiverr are the titans of the industry, acting as a massive digital bazaar connecting freelancers with clients for projects ranging from a five-minute voice-over to a six-month software development contract. The primary advantage of these platforms is volume. There is a constant stream of new projects being posted, offering a clear path for a newcomer to land their first few clients and begin building a track record. They also handle the administrative side of things, providing a built-in system for proposals, contracts, and, most importantly, payments, which removes a significant amount of stress.

However, these marketplaces come with significant downsides. The competition is fierce and global, which can create a "race to the bottom" on pricing, especially for more commoditized skills. It can be difficult to stand out from the crowd, and the platforms take a substantial percentage of your earnings in fees, sometimes as much as twenty percent. Furthermore, you are building your professional reputation on rented land. Your profile, your reviews, and your work history are all tied to the platform. If the platform changes its algorithm or you decide to leave, you can't easily take that hard-won reputation with you. These sites are best viewed as a launchpad, not a long-term home.

A smarter strategy is to also focus on niche job boards. Whatever your specialty, there is likely a community or website dedicated to it that features a job board. The ProBlogger job board is a goldmine for writers. Dribbble and Behance have robust job sections for designers and creatives. AngelList is the go-to for roles at startups, many of which are remote. The leads on these niche sites are often of higher quality, the competition is more focused, and you are connecting with employers who are already looking for your specific skill set.

The Warm Introduction: Leveraging Your Personal and Professional Network

While job boards are a necessary tool, they are fundamentally a numbers game. You are often one of hundreds of applicants, and your resume can easily get lost in the digital shuffle. The single most effective strategy for bypassing the queue and landing a great role is leveraging your existing network. People hire people they know, like, and trust. Your warmest leads will almost always come from a personal connection or referral. The problem is that most people approach this process backwards, either by not reaching out at all or by asking for a job directly, which can put their contacts in an awkward position.

The first step is a strategic announcement. You cannot expect your network to read your mind. You must proactively inform them of your new direction. This doesn't have to be a grand declaration. It can be a simple, well-crafted post on LinkedIn or a personal email to former colleagues, mentors, and friends. The key is to be specific and to ask for information, not a job. Your message should be clear about the services you are now offering or the type of remote role you are seeking. Instead of saying, "Do you know anyone who is hiring?" try, "I'm now focusing on freelance content marketing for B2B tech companies. If you know anyone who is struggling to get their company blog off the ground, I'd be grateful for an introduction."

LinkedIn is your most powerful tool in this endeavor. It is your digital resume, your professional network, and your personal branding platform all in one. Start by optimizing your profile. Your headline should be a clear statement of who you are and what you do, such as "Remote Senior Project Manager" or "Freelance Python Developer for FinTech." Fill out your "About" section with a compelling narrative that highlights your skills and your suitability for remote work, emphasizing traits like self-management and strong communication. Actively seek out and connect with recruiters, hiring managers, and department heads at companies you admire, especially those that are known to be remote-friendly.

Do not just use LinkedIn as a static profile. Use it as a networking tool. Engage with the content your connections are posting. Share articles and insights related to your field of expertise. This demonstrates your knowledge and keeps you top-of-mind. When you see that a company on your target list is hiring, look for a first or second-degree connection who works there. Reaching out for an informational interview or a brief chat about the company culture is far more effective than applying cold. A referral from an existing employee can be the golden ticket that gets your application moved to the top of the pile.

Forging Your Own Path: The Direct Pitch and Cold Outreach

Waiting for jobs to be posted or for referrals to come your way is a passive strategy. The most proactive and often highest-reward approach is to go directly to the source. This involves identifying companies or clients you want to work with and reaching out to them directly, regardless of whether they have a job opening advertised. This strategy requires more research and courage, but it allows you to bypass the competition entirely and create an opportunity where none existed before. It positions you not as a job seeker, but as a problem solver.

For those seeking remote employment, start by creating a "dream company" list. Research and identify twenty to thirty companies whose mission you admire, whose products you love, and whose culture seems aligned with your values. Focus on companies that are already remote-first or have a significant remote workforce. Follow them on LinkedIn and other social media, and set up alerts for any news or announcements. The goal is to become an expert on these companies. Then, identify the key decision-makers in the department where you'd like to work. The goal is not to spam them with your resume, but to find a way to provide value and build a relationship over time.

For freelancers, this strategy takes the form of the "cold pitch." This is not about sending a generic, copy-and-pasted email to a hundred businesses. A successful cold pitch is a highly targeted, well-researched, and value-driven piece of communication. The process begins with identifying a potential client and then finding a specific problem you can solve for them. Perhaps you notice their website loads slowly, their blog hasn't been updated in six months, or their social media presence is inconsistent.

Your pitch should be concise and structured. Start by introducing yourself briefly, then immediately pivot to the problem you have identified, showing that you have done your homework. Crucially, you should then offer a tangible suggestion or a piece of high-level advice for free. This demonstrates your expertise and builds goodwill. Only then should you briefly mention that you provide services to help implement these kinds of solutions and suggest a brief call to discuss further. This approach transforms you from an unsolicited vendor into a valuable consultant. Even if it doesn't lead to immediate work, a thoughtful pitch can put you on their radar for future projects.

Becoming a Magnet: Using Inbound Strategies to Attract Opportunities

The strategies discussed so far have been outbound; they involve you actively reaching out to find work. The ultimate long-term goal is to reverse this dynamic. You want to build a professional reputation and an online presence so strong that the best clients and employers start coming to you. This is the inbound approach, where you act as a magnet for opportunities. While it takes more time and effort upfront, it is the key to creating a truly sustainable and high-quality pipeline of work.

The core of an inbound strategy is content and community. You need to create a professional "home" on the internet that is not a social media platform. This could be a personal portfolio website or a professional blog. As we will discuss in the next chapter, your portfolio is your primary sales tool, but it can also be a lead generation engine if it is optimized for search engines and showcases your expertise effectively. Writing blog posts about common challenges in your industry, creating case studies of your past work, or sharing your unique perspective on emerging trends can establish you as a thought leader.

Beyond your own website, become an active and genuinely helpful member of the online communities where your ideal clients or employers spend their time. This could be a specific subreddit, a niche Slack channel, a professional association's online forum, or a relevant Facebook group. The key is to contribute, not to broadcast. Answer people's questions, offer thoughtful advice, and share valuable resources without any expectation of immediate return. People will begin to recognize you as a knowledgeable and helpful expert in your field. Over time, these organic interactions naturally lead to conversations about your work and, eventually, to direct opportunities.

This inbound strategy is a slow burn, but it yields the highest quality leads. The clients and employers who find you through your content or your community contributions are already convinced of your expertise and are more likely to be a good fit. They are coming to you because of your reputation, which puts you in a much stronger negotiating position than when you are one of fifty applicants for a freelance gig on Upwork.

The search for remote work is not a linear process. It is a continuous cycle of prospecting, networking, and building your personal brand. The most successful digital nomads are disciplined in their approach. They dedicate a certain amount of time each week to their business development activities, even when they are busy with client work. They might spend an hour on job boards, thirty minutes engaging on LinkedIn, and an hour writing a blog post. They track their leads and are persistent in their follow-up. They understand that rejection is not personal; it is simply part of the process. By combining these different strategies, you move from a position of scarcity to one of abundance, creating a robust and resilient system for finding the best opportunities from anywhere in the world.

CHAPTER SEVEN: Building a Standout Portfolio and Winning Proposals

The strategies in the previous chapter have filled your pipeline. Your inbox has a promising lead, a job board application has received a response, or a networking connection has made an introduction. A potential client or employer is now looking your way, asking the implicit but crucial question: "Are you the right person for this job?" This is the moment of truth, the pivot point where opportunity is either won or lost. Finding the lead is the science; winning it is the art. Your success in this critical stage hinges on two key assets: your portfolio and your proposal.

These are not mere administrative hurdles to clear. They are your primary tools of persuasion. A standout portfolio acts as your silent salesperson, working around the clock to showcase your expertise and prove your capabilities. A winning proposal is your direct pitch, the conversational bridge that transforms a potential client's problem into your paid project. Mastering the creation of both is not just about landing a single gig; it's about building a repeatable system that will consistently convert interest into income, providing the financial engine for your nomadic life. This chapter is a blueprint for forging these essential tools, moving you from a hopeful applicant to the undeniable choice.

Your portfolio is the most powerful piece of marketing material you will ever create. It is the tangible proof of the skills you listed on your LinkedIn profile and the claims you made in your outreach email. In the remote world, where an in-person handshake and a confident first impression are impossible, your portfolio does the heavy lifting. It's the ultimate embodiment of the golden rule: "Show, don't tell." Anyone can claim to be a "creative graphic designer" or a "results-driven marketer." The professional who lands the job is the one who can immediately follow that claim with a link to a body of work that leaves no room for doubt.

Think of your portfolio not as an archive of everything you have ever done, but as a curated gallery of your greatest hits. Its purpose is not to be comprehensive, but to be compelling. A client or hiring manager is a busy person, and they will likely spend only a few minutes glancing at your work. Your job is to make those minutes count. This means that quality will always triumph over quantity. A portfolio with three exceptional, in-depth case studies will be infinitely more effective than one with twenty mediocre screenshots of past projects. Each piece you choose to include should be a testament to your skill, your professionalism, and the value you bring to a project.

The ideal home for your portfolio is a personal website under your own domain name (e.g., www.yourname.com). While platforms like Behance for designers or GitHub for developers are excellent for showcasing work within those specific communities, a personal website gives you complete control over the narrative. It is your owned-and-operated digital storefront. You can design it to reflect your personal brand, structure it to guide visitors through a carefully crafted story, and integrate elements like a blog or testimonials to build further authority. It signals a level of professionalism and long-term commitment that a simple social media profile cannot match.

The structure of your portfolio website should be simple, intuitive, and focused on the user's journey. At a minimum, it needs four key sections. The first is, of course, your work. This is the main event. The second is a clear and engaging "About Me" page. This is your chance to tell your story, to connect on a human level, and to highlight the soft skills that make you an excellent remote collaborator—communication, self-discipline, and reliability. The third is a page for testimonials or social proof. Positive quotes from past clients or managers are invaluable for building trust. Finally, and most obviously, you need a prominent and easy-to-use contact page, making it frictionless for an impressed visitor to get in touch.

The heart of an effective portfolio, however, is not just displaying the final product. It is telling the story behind it. This is where the power of the case study comes in. A case study transforms a simple image or a link into a compelling business narrative. Instead of just showing the beautiful website you designed, you walk the potential client through the entire process. You start by outlining the client's initial problem or goal (The Situation). You then define your specific role and responsibilities in the project (The Task). Next, you detail the steps you took—the research, the strategy, the creative process—to solve the problem (The Action). Finally, and most critically, you showcase the outcome with concrete, measurable results (The Result).

For example, a content writer's case study wouldn't just link to a blog post. It would state: "My client, a B2B software company, was struggling to generate leads from their blog. I developed a content strategy focused on long-tail keywords and created a series of in-depth articles. This resulted in a 300% increase in organic traffic to their blog within six months and a 45% increase in marketing qualified leads." This focus on results shifts the conversation from your skills to the value you create. You are no longer just a writer; you are a business growth partner. This is an infinitely more powerful position.

But what if you are just starting out? The classic dilemma is needing a portfolio to get work, but needing work to build a portfolio. This is a hurdle, but it is far from insurmountable. The solution is to create your own experience. The first and most effective strategy is to undertake self-initiated or "spec" projects. If you are a web designer, find a local non-profit with a dated website and redesign it from the ground up as a passion project. If you are a copywriter, pick a brand you admire and write a series of advertisements or a new landing page for them. These projects demonstrate your skills, your initiative, and your creative thinking just as effectively as paid work.

Another powerful strategy is to offer your services for a reduced rate, or even pro-bono, for a very limited number of initial clients. Reach out to small businesses, non-profits, or even friends and family who could benefit from your skills. Be explicit that you are doing this in exchange for a portfolio piece and a detailed testimonial. This is a short-term investment in your long-term marketing assets. The key is to treat these projects with the same level of professionalism and dedication as you would a high-paying client. The quality of your first portfolio pieces will set the standard for the kind of work you attract in the future.

Once your portfolio is polished and ready, it becomes the foundation for your proposals. If the portfolio is the evidence, the proposal is the argument. It is your direct response to a client's specific need, and it is where you connect the dots between their problem and your proven ability to solve it. The single greatest mistake made in writing proposals is treating them like a generic resume or a price list. A winning proposal is not about you; it is about them. It is a document of empathy, demonstrating that you have listened, you understand their challenge, and you have a clear plan to help them succeed.

This requires a fundamental shift in approach. Every proposal you send should be a bespoke document, meticulously tailored to the specific project and client. The age of the copy-and-pasted template is over. While you can certainly have a basic framework, the content must be deeply personalized. This starts with the opening line. Address the client by name. Reference a specific detail from their project description or something you noticed on their company website. This simple act immediately shows that you are not just blasting out dozens of generic applications, but have taken the time to engage with their specific situation.

The structure of your proposal should guide the client on a logical journey. Begin not with a long-winded introduction about yourself, but by restating their problem in your own words. This is called "framing the problem." It demonstrates that you have paid attention and validates their needs. For example: "From your project description, I understand you're looking for a skilled video editor to turn your raw podcast footage into engaging, shareable clips for social media, with the goal of increasing your audience engagement and driving traffic back to the full episodes." This immediately builds rapport and establishes you as a thoughtful partner.

Only after you have demonstrated your understanding of the problem should you present your solution. This is where you outline your proposed process. Avoid getting bogged down in excessive technical detail. Instead, break your approach down into clear, logical phases or steps. For instance: "My process for this would involve three key phases: 1) A kickoff call to discuss your brand's style guide and content pillars, 2) The initial editing of one pilot clip for your review and feedback, and 3) The weekly delivery of five polished video clips based on the approved style." This clarity gives the client confidence that you are an organized professional with a structured plan, not just someone who will "wing it."

This is also the perfect moment to seamlessly integrate your portfolio. As you outline your solution, you can directly reference past projects that are relevant to the client's needs. This is far more effective than simply including a generic link at the end of your message. You can write something like, "This process is similar to the one I used for the ABC Podcast, where my video clips helped increase their Instagram engagement by 80% over three months. You can see an example of that work here." This provides immediate, relevant proof of your ability to deliver the exact results the client is looking for.

When it comes to pricing, clarity and confidence are key. Avoid simply stating a single, flat number without context. Instead, frame your pricing in terms of the value you are providing. One effective technique is to offer two or three tiered packages. This shifts the client's thinking from "Should I hire this person?" to "Which of their options is best for me?" It gives them a sense of control and allows you to anchor your value at a higher price point. For each package, clearly define the deliverables and the outcome. For example, a "Starter Package" might include five video clips, while a "Growth Package" could include ten clips plus thumbnail design and caption writing.

Whenever possible, opt for project-based pricing over hourly rates. Charging by the hour incentivizes inefficiency and forces you to justify your time. Project-based pricing focuses the client on the final result and the value you are delivering. You are being paid for your expertise and the outcome, not for the minutes you spend at a keyboard. This positions you as a professional consultant, not a temporary worker. Be prepared to explain how you arrived at your price, tying it back to the scope of work and the value it will create for their business.

Finally, every proposal must end with a clear and unambiguous call to action. You have done the work to build trust and present a compelling solution; do not leave the client wondering what to do next. Make the next step easy and low-commitment. Instead of a vague "I look forward to hearing from you," be specific: "If this proposal aligns with what you're looking for, the next step would be a brief 15-minute introductory call to discuss the project in more detail and answer any questions you might have. Does Tuesday or Thursday afternoon work for you?" This takes the burden of decision-making off the client and moves the process forward.

Of course, there are common pitfalls to avoid. The most glaring is a lack of proofreading. A proposal riddled with typos and grammatical errors screams a lack of attention to detail, which is the last impression you want to give. Always read your proposal aloud before sending it to catch any awkward phrasing. Another common mistake is being too vague. Clearly define the scope of work, what is included, and, just as importantly, what is not. This prevents "scope creep" down the line and sets clear expectations from the outset. Finally, resist the urge to compete on price. There will always be someone cheaper, especially in a global marketplace. Instead, compete on value, expertise, and the quality of your proposed solution.

Your portfolio and your proposal process are not static documents; they are dynamic assets that should evolve with your career. After you complete a successful project, update your portfolio with a new case study. If you find that a certain part of your proposal is consistently confusing to clients, refine it. This continuous process of improvement will turn your client acquisition efforts from a stressful, scattershot activity into a well-oiled machine. It is this system that will provide you with the consistent workflow and financial freedom required to not just travel the world, but to build a thriving, sustainable career from anywhere within it.

CHAPTER EIGHT: Financial Planning for the Location Independent

We have arrived at the most practical and, for many, the most intimidating chapter in this handbook. The previous sections have dealt with mindset, skills, and finding work—the components that build your capability. This chapter deals with the fuel that makes the entire nomadic engine run: your money. Without a firm grasp of your finances, the dream of location independence can quickly curdle into a stressful, hand-to-mouth existence. The freedom you seek is not just about geography; it is, at its core, financial. It is the freedom from the anxiety of an unexpected bill, the freedom to choose your next destination without being dictated by a depleted bank account, and the freedom to build a sustainable future while living an extraordinary present.

Financial planning for a digital nomad is a fundamentally different beast than traditional personal finance. The old playbook of a stable monthly salary, a predictable mortgage payment, and a 401(k) tied to a single employer simply does not apply. Your income might be variable, your expenses will change with every border crossing, and your financial life will span multiple currencies. This requires a new mindset, one that embraces flexibility, prioritizes cash flow, and treats your financial plan not as a rigid set of rules, but as a dynamic, adaptable strategy. This is not about deprivation or obsessive penny-pinching; it is about conscious spending and strategic allocation. It is about building a system that empowers your lifestyle, rather than being constrained by it.

The Freedom Fund: Your Financial Launchpad

Before you book a single flight or give notice at your current job, you must build a financial runway. This is non-negotiable. Attempting to start this lifestyle without a significant cash buffer is like trying to fly a plane while simultaneously building the wings. The stress of having to generate income immediately under the pressure of dwindling funds is the number one killer of nomadic dreams. This buffer is your "Freedom Fund." Its name is intentional; this money buys you the freedom to make good decisions, the freedom to say no to bad clients, and the freedom to handle a crisis without having to book a flight home.

The standard advice for a traditional lifestyle is to have three to six months of living expenses saved in an emergency fund. For a digital nomad, this is the absolute minimum, and a more conservative approach is highly recommended. Your Freedom Fund needs to cover more than just your basic living costs. It should be calculated to include several distinct components. First, calculate your baseline monthly burn rate—the absolute minimum you need to live on. Multiply this by at least six. This is the core of your fund.

Next, add a "Get Home" buffer. This is a dedicated pot of money sufficient to buy a last-minute, one-way flight back to your home country from anywhere in the world, plus enough to cover your expenses for a month while you get back on your feet. The psychological comfort this provides is immeasurable. Then, add a "Setup Cost" fund. This covers the initial, one-time expenses of starting your journey: a new piece of gear, visa application fees, a security deposit on your first long-term stay, and comprehensive travel insurance. Finally, if you are a freelancer, add a "Business Buffer" to cover at least one month of business expenses and a potential dry spell with no new client work.

It might look something like this: (6 x Monthly Expenses) + (Emergency Flight + 1 Month Home Expenses) + (Initial Gear + Visa Costs) + (1 Month Business Expenses). This may seem like a daunting number, and it will take time and discipline to save. But every dollar you add to this fund is a brick in the foundation of your new life. This money should be kept in a high-yield savings account that is liquid and easily accessible. It is not an investment fund to be risked in the market; it is your insurance policy against the inherent uncertainty of the road.

The Art of the Dynamic Budget

For a digital nomad, a traditional, static budget is a useless artifact. Setting a fixed amount for "groceries" or "transportation" is meaningless when the cost of a meal in Thailand is a fraction of what it is in Switzerland. Your budget cannot be a rigid spreadsheet you create once and then follow blindly. It must be a living, breathing document that adapts to your location. This is the art of the dynamic budget.

The most effective approach is to think in terms of percentages and to track your spending religiously. Instead of fixed dollar amounts, you might aim to allocate your monthly income along these lines: 50% for living expenses (accommodation, food, transport), 20% for savings and investments, 15% for business expenses and taxes, and 15% for "fun" and discretionary spending. The actual dollar amounts will fluctuate, but the proportional allocation provides a consistent framework.

The cornerstone of a successful nomad budget is research. Before you decide on a new destination, you must become an expert on its cost of living. Websites like Nomad List and Numbeo are invaluable resources, providing crowdsourced data on everything from the average cost of a one-bedroom apartment to the price of a cappuccino in thousands of cities worldwide. Use these as a starting point, but supplement them with on-the-ground research in expat forums and Facebook groups for your target destination. Ask specific questions: "What is a realistic monthly budget for a single person in Medellin who enjoys eating out a few times a week?" The answers you get will be far more nuanced than any generic online calculator.

This research allows you to practice one of the greatest financial superpowers of a digital nomad: geoarbitrage. In simple terms, geoarbitrage is the practice of earning an income in a strong currency (like the US Dollar or the Euro) while living and spending in a country with a much lower cost of living. Earning a San Francisco salary while paying Southeast Asian prices is the fastest way to supercharge your savings and dramatically improve your quality of life. This strategic selection of destinations is the most powerful lever you have to control your expenses.

To manage your dynamic budget, you will need a robust tracking system. A simple spreadsheet can work, but a dedicated budgeting app is often more effective. Apps like Trail Wallet, Mint, or You Need a Budget (YNAB) can sync with your bank accounts, categorize your spending automatically, and provide a clear picture of where your money is going in real-time. The habit of tracking every single expense, no matter how small, is crucial in the beginning. It provides the data you need to understand your own spending patterns and to make informed decisions about your budget.

Taming the Income Roller Coaster

If you are a remote employee with a steady paycheck, you can skip ahead. For the freelancers and entrepreneurs among us, however, managing a variable income is the central financial challenge. The "feast or famine" cycle is a well-known phenomenon, and without a system to manage it, it can lead to a chaotic and stressful financial life. The key is to create a buffer between your incoming revenue and your personal spending. You should not live directly out of your business account.

The most effective method is to "pay yourself" a fixed, regular salary, just as a traditional company would. This requires a two-step process. First, every single payment you receive from a client goes directly into a dedicated business bank account. Do not touch this money for personal expenses. Second, on a set schedule (for example, the 1st and 15th of every month), you transfer a predetermined "salary" from your business account to your personal checking account. This is the only money you are allowed to spend on your personal living expenses for that period.

This salary should be based on your conservative monthly budget, not on your best-case income scenario. The excess money that remains in the business account during a "feast" month is your buffer against the "famine" months. This system smooths out the peaks and valleys of your income, creating the predictability and stability that is essential for long-term financial planning. It breaks the psychological link between a big client payment and an immediate spending spree, fostering a more disciplined and professional approach to your finances.

A more advanced version of this is the "bucket" or "percentage" system. With this method, you create several different business savings accounts, each for a specific purpose. Every time a client payment comes in, you immediately allocate a percentage of it to each bucket. A common allocation might be: 30% into a "Tax" account, 10% into a "Business Reinvestment" account (for new software, courses, etc.), 20% into a "Profit" or "Long-Term Savings" account, and the remaining 40% into your "Operating Expenses" account, from which you will pay yourself your salary. This automated allocation ensures that you are always setting aside money for your obligations and future goals before you have a chance to spend it.

Future-Proofing Your Finances: Saving and Investing on the Move

One of the most persistent and damaging myths about the digital nomad lifestyle is that it is an extended vacation, incompatible with long-term financial goals like retirement. This is a dangerous fallacy. A life of travel is not a hall pass to neglect your future self. In fact, thanks to strategies like geoarbitrage, many nomads find they can save and invest far more aggressively than they ever could in their high-cost-of-living home countries. The principles of sound long-term planning do not change just because your address does.

The golden rule of saving and investing is to automate it. The moment your "salary" hits your personal account, an automatic transfer should be set up to whisk a portion of it away to your savings and investment accounts. This "pay yourself first" principle is even more critical when you are surrounded by the temptations of new and exciting experiences. By making your savings automatic, you remove the need for willpower. The money is saved before you even have the chance to consider spending it on another weekend trip.

The specifics of where and how to invest can be complex for nomads, as many financial institutions have residency requirements. This is an area where it is often wise to seek advice from a financial planner who specializes in working with expatriates. However, the general goal is to continue contributing to tax-advantaged retirement accounts in your home country for as long as you are legally able to. If that is not possible, opening a taxable international brokerage account is often the next best step. The key is to keep investing consistently in low-cost, diversified index funds or ETFs. The power of compound interest is a global phenomenon; it works just as well from a beach in Portugal as it does from a suburb in Ohio.

The Currency Game: Making Your Money Work Globally

Living a multi-country life means you will be operating in a multi-currency world. Navigating this landscape inefficiently can lead to a slow and silent drain on your finances, with hundreds or even thousands of dollars lost each year to hidden fees. The three main culprits are foreign transaction fees, ATM withdrawal fees, and unfavorable currency exchange rates. Winning the currency game is about finding the right financial tools to minimize these costs.

First, you must have a credit card that does not charge foreign transaction fees. These fees are typically 1-3% of every single purchase you make abroad, a completely unnecessary tax on your existence. Many travel-focused credit cards waive this fee. Second, you need a debit card that offers free or reimbursed international ATM withdrawals. Relying on local ATMs is often the cheapest way to get local cash, but only if your home bank isn't charging you a hefty fee for the privilege. We will explore the specific types of bank accounts that offer these features in the next chapter.

Finally, you must be wary of "dynamic currency conversion." This is a common trap you will encounter at shops and ATMs, where you are offered the "convenience" of being charged in your home currency. Always decline this offer and choose to be charged in the local currency. The exchange rate offered by the local merchant is almost always significantly worse than the rate your own bank will give you, and this "convenience" is a well-disguised and costly fee.

Your Financial Armor: The Critical Role of Insurance

No financial plan is complete without a robust defense. For a digital nomad, your primary defense against a catastrophic financial event is insurance. This is not a luxury or an optional add-on; it is as essential as your passport and your laptop. A serious medical emergency in a foreign country can lead to devastating, life-altering bills. A stolen laptop can instantly cripple your ability to earn an income. Proper insurance is your financial armor against the worst-case scenarios.

Your top priority is comprehensive travel medical insurance. This is not the same as the basic trip insurance you might buy for a one-week vacation. You need a plan specifically designed for long-term travelers and digital nomads that covers emergency medical care, hospitalization, and, most critically, medical evacuation to a suitable facility or back to your home country. Companies like SafetyWing and World Nomads specialize in this type of coverage. The monthly premium for such a plan is a small, predictable business expense that protects you from a potentially bankrupting medical event.

Beyond health, you should strongly consider insuring your gear. Your laptop, camera, and phone are the tools of your trade. A dedicated gear insurance policy can cover them against theft, loss, and accidental damage. This ensures that a single unfortunate incident does not derail your ability to work. Considering the cost and importance of your electronics, this small annual expense provides invaluable peace of mind.

Ultimately, solid financial planning is the silent partner in your nomadic adventure. It is the work you do behind the scenes that makes the highlight reel possible. It is about building a system of conscious choices, automated habits, and protective measures that gives you the confidence to fully embrace the freedom you have worked so hard to create.

CHAPTER NINE: Navigating Taxes and Banking as a Global Citizen

If the digital nomad lifestyle were a blockbuster movie, this chapter would be the scene where the lights come up, the credits roll, and the stadium cleaners start sweeping up the popcorn. It lacks the glamour of landing in a new country or the thrill of a successful project, but without it, the entire production falls apart. We're talking about taxes and banking—the unsexy, intimidating, yet absolutely critical infrastructure that makes a sustainable nomadic life possible. Ignoring this side of things is the fastest way to turn your global adventure into a bureaucratic nightmare with serious financial consequences.

This chapter is designed to be your plain-language guide to these complex topics. It is not, and should not be considered, professional legal or financial advice. Tax laws are labyrinthine, country-specific, and change constantly. The single most important piece of advice within these pages is to hire a qualified professional, ideally an accountant who specializes in expatriate or location-independent tax matters. Think of this chapter as your orientation, a way to learn the right questions to ask and to build a strategic framework for managing your money as a citizen of the world. Getting this right allows your financial life to hum quietly in the background, freeing you up to focus on the work and the world in front of you.

Let's begin by dispelling a pervasive and dangerous myth: the idea that by being constantly on the move, you can somehow exist in a magical, tax-free limbo. This is a fantasy. You cannot simply opt out of the tax system. As the saying goes, only two things in life are certain, and the one we're discussing here is a global reality. Every country has a set of rules for determining who owes them money, and your goal is not to evade these rules but to understand and navigate them legally and efficiently. Your tax obligations are typically tied to two key concepts: your citizenship and your tax residency.

For citizens of the United States, the system is unique and unyielding. The U.S. operates on a system of citizenship-based taxation. This means that if you are a U.S. citizen or a green card holder, you are required to file a U.S. federal tax return and report your worldwide income every single year, regardless of where you live or where that income was earned. It doesn't matter if you haven't set foot on American soil in a decade; Uncle Sam still expects to hear from you. This is a fundamental, non-negotiable reality for American nomads.

Most other countries in the world use a residency-based system of taxation. In this model, a country only has the right to tax your worldwide income if you are considered a "tax resident" there. If you are not a tax resident, you may still owe tax on income sourced from within that country, but not on your global earnings. This is where things become a complex dance of days and details. Each country has its own set of tests to determine tax residency. The most common is the 183-day rule: if you spend more than 183 days (roughly six months) in a single country during its tax year, you are often automatically considered a tax resident for that year.

However, the 183-day rule is often just the beginning. Many countries also use qualitative tests, such as determining where you have your "center of vital interests." This looks at factors like where your primary home is, where your close family lives, and where your main economic ties are. For nomads from residency-based countries like Canada, the UK, or Australia, it is possible to officially sever tax residency with your home country, but this is a serious legal step. It often involves proving that you have established more significant ties elsewhere and have truly and permanently left. It is not as simple as just being out of the country for a certain number of days and requires meticulous planning with a tax professional.

For American nomads, who cannot simply sever their tax obligations, the key is not to avoid filing but to use the legal provisions designed for citizens abroad to reduce their tax liability, often to zero. The most powerful of these tools is the Foreign Earned Income Exclusion (FEIE). This provision allows eligible taxpayers to exclude a significant portion of their foreign-earned income from U.S. income tax. The exclusion amount is indexed for inflation and is over $120,000 for the 2023 tax year. To qualify, you must have foreign earned income, your tax home must be in a foreign country, and you must meet either the Bona Fide Residence Test or the Physical Presence Test.

The Bona Fide Residence Test is for those who have established a more permanent life in a foreign country for an entire tax year. For most nomads, the more relevant and straightforward option is the Physical Presence Test. To meet this test, you must be physically present in a foreign country or countries for at least 330 full days during any consecutive 12-month period. Those 330 days do not have to be consecutive; they just have to fall within that rolling 12-month window. This requires precise tracking of your travel days, as even a single day short can disqualify you. It's important to note that the FEIE only applies to *earned income* (like freelance earnings or a salary), not to *unearned income* from sources like interest, dividends, or capital gains.

Even if you qualify for the FEIE, your tax journey isn't over. You might also be able to claim the Foreign Housing Exclusion or Deduction for housing expenses above a certain base amount. Furthermore, even if the FEIE reduces your income tax to zero, you may still be liable for U.S. self-employment taxes (Social Security and Medicare), which is a significant consideration for freelancers and entrepreneurs. This is where things get complicated with "Totalization Agreements"—treaties between the U.S. and other countries designed to avoid double taxation of social security contributions.

This brings us to the broader topic of tax treaties. Most developed nations have entered into double-taxation agreements with one another. The purpose of these treaties is to prevent the same income from being taxed by two different countries. They contain complex "tie-breaker" rules to determine which country gets primary taxing rights when an individual might be considered a resident of both. While you don't need to become an expert on international tax law, it is important to be aware that these treaties exist and can significantly impact your situation. An accountant specializing in this field will be able to navigate these treaties on your behalf.

Finally, remember that your tax obligations are not limited to your home country. As mentioned, spending more than 183 days in another country can make you a tax resident there, creating a local filing obligation. This is a crucial intersection of tax law and visa law (which we will cover in Chapter Ten). Working on a tourist visa is often illegal, and even with a digital nomad visa, you need to understand the local tax implications. Some digital nomad visas come with a flat, preferential tax rate, while others will subject you to the standard resident tax rates after a certain period. Never assume; always verify the local rules.

To manage this complexity, you need a clear, practical strategy. First and foremost, hire a professional. The money you spend on a qualified expat tax accountant will pay for itself many times over in peace of mind and potential tax savings. They are your guide through the labyrinth. Second, become a fanatical record-keeper. Use a spreadsheet or an app to track your physical location for every single day of the year. This is your proof for the Physical Presence Test or for demonstrating non-residency elsewhere. Keep meticulous records of all your income and business expenses, just as you would at home.

Third, use the "tax bucket" system discussed in the previous chapter. Create a separate savings account labeled "Taxes." Every time you receive a payment from a client or your employer, immediately transfer a conservative percentage (a good starting point is 25-30%) into this account. This money is not yours; it belongs to the government. Do not touch it. When tax time comes, you will have the funds ready, avoiding the panic of a large, unexpected bill. This single habit is one of the most powerful stress-reducers for any self-employed person, nomad or not.

With the tax puzzle framed, we can turn to its operational counterpart: banking. An inefficient banking setup will bleed you dry through a thousand tiny cuts of fees and poor exchange rates.

A smart, streamlined setup, on the other hand, becomes a powerful enabler of your lifestyle. The ideal system for a digital nomad isn't a single "super-bank," but a strategic combination of different tools, what we can call the Nomad's Banking Trinity. This consists of a solid home base bank, a global currency account, and, when needed, a local bank account.

Your home base bank is your anchor. This should be an account in your home country that is genuinely "nomad-friendly." This means it has a robust and secure online banking portal and mobile app, because you will never be walking into a physical branch. Crucially, it should offer a debit card with no foreign transaction fees and, ideally, refunds for ATM fees charged by other banks worldwide. In the United States, Charles Schwab Bank's High-Yield Investor Checking account is a legendary favorite among nomads for exactly this reason: it charges no foreign transaction fees and provides unlimited rebates for ATM fees from any machine, anywhere in the world. Look for similar features from banks in your home country. This account is where you might receive your primary income and keep the bulk of your Freedom Fund.

The second piece of the trinity, and the true game-changer for modern nomads, is a global currency account from a financial technology (FinTech) company. Services like Wise (formerly TransferWise) and Revolut are not traditional banks but are designed from the ground up for people who live and work across borders. Their primary function is to act as the circulatory system for your global finances. With an account like Wise, you can hold balances in dozens of different currencies simultaneously. It provides you with local bank details (like an IBAN for Europe or a routing number for the US), allowing you to get paid like a local in multiple countries.

The killer feature of these services is the ability to convert and send money internationally at the mid-market exchange rate—the real rate you see on Google—for a tiny, transparent fee. This is a massive improvement over traditional banks, which often hide hefty markups in their exchange rates. These services also come with a debit card, allowing you to spend directly from your foreign currency balances with no fees. This means you can convert USD to Euros in your Wise app when the rate is good, and then use your Wise card to pay for dinner in Lisbon, spending those Euros directly. It's a powerful tool for managing currency fluctuations and avoiding fees.

The final, and most situational, part of the trinity is a local bank account. If you plan to stay in a country for an extended period (six months or more), opening an account with a local bank can sometimes be a necessity. It can make life much easier for things like paying rent and utility bills, which may be difficult to do from a foreign account. It can also be required if you are working with local clients who prefer to pay via local bank transfer. Be aware that opening a local account as a foreigner can range from straightforward to a bureaucratic marathon, often requiring a specific type of visa, proof of address, and a great deal of patience.

Once you have these tools in place, your financial workflow becomes simple and efficient. A client pays an invoice in US dollars into your US home base bank account. You then use Wise to pull that money from your US account and transfer it to your Wise multi-currency account, converting the portion you need for living expenses into Thai Baht. You use your Wise debit card for most of your daily spending in Thailand. When you need cash, you use your Charles Schwab debit card at a local ATM to withdraw Baht, knowing that any fees will be automatically refunded at the end of the month. Your money moves seamlessly and cheaply across borders.

To make this system resilient, you must build in redundancy. Never, ever rely on a single card. A lost wallet, a stolen card, or a bank's fraud detection system freezing your account can leave you stranded. You should carry at least three cards: two debit cards from different banks and at least one credit card. Keep them in separate physical locations—one in your wallet, a backup in the hidden pocket of your backpack, and another spare locked in your apartment. It's also wise to carry cards on different payment networks (e.g., one Visa and one Mastercard), as some merchants may not accept one or the other.

Finally, a quick word on security. Before you leave, set up travel notices with all your banks and credit card companies. Even if they claim their systems are smart enough not to need them, do it anyway. It's a five-minute task that can prevent your account from being frozen when it detects a transaction from a new country. More importantly, you must solve the two-factor authentication (2FA) problem. Many banks insist on sending a verification code via SMS to your registered phone number, which is a major issue when that SIM card is from a country you left three months ago. Whenever possible, switch your 2FA method to an app-based authenticator like Google Authenticator or Authy. These apps generate codes directly on your phone, independent of your cellular service, ensuring you can always access your financial accounts securely from anywhere in the world.

CHAPTER TEN: Visas and Legalities: The Practical Guide to Working Abroad

We have now entered the domain of the single greatest logistical hurdle and source of anxiety for aspiring digital nomads. Visas. The word itself can conjure images of endless paperwork, bureaucratic indifference, and the arbitrary power of a single stamp. For all the freedom that technology affords, the world is still a place of hard borders and strict rules. The ability to work from anywhere is a modern reality, but the legal frameworks of most countries are still catching up. Navigating this landscape is the ultimate test of your planning, patience, and commitment.

This chapter is a practical guide, not a collection of clever loopholes or "hacks." The goal is to build a sustainable, long-term nomadic life, and that requires a foundation of legality. Operating in a legal gray area might work for a few months, but it's a stressful and precarious way to live, always accompanied by the low-grade fear of being caught, fined, or banned from a country you love. Understanding the legal pathways available to you is about more than just following the rules; it's about giving yourself the peace of mind to truly enjoy your freedom.

First, we must deconstruct the concept of "work." When you sit in a café in Lisbon, earning money from a client in Chicago, are you "working in Portugal"? From your perspective, you are simply working online. From the perspective of the Portuguese government, however, the answer is more complicated. A country's immigration and labor laws are designed primarily to protect its local job market and to collect tax revenue. When you are physically present in their country and engaging in economic activity, you fall under their jurisdiction, even if your employer is a continent away. This is the fundamental tension that a digital nomad must navigate: your work is global, but your physical body is always subject to local law.

This brings us to the most common, and most perilous, strategy employed by new and experienced nomads alike: working remotely while on a tourist visa. Let's be unequivocally clear: in the vast majority of countries, this is technically illegal. A tourist visa or a visa-free entry stamp is granted for the express purpose of leisure and tourism. It explicitly forbids engaging in any form of work. When an immigration officer asks the purpose of your visit, and you are on a tourist entry, the correct and honest answer is "tourism." Lying to an immigration official is a serious offense with severe consequences.

The reality, of course, is that hundreds of thousands of nomads operate in this gray area. They enter a country as a tourist, quietly work on their laptops for a US-based company, spend their foreign-earned money in the local economy, and leave before their tourist stay expires without issue. The risk in this "don't ask, don't tell" approach lies in the "don't get caught" part. While the chances of a government actively hunting for nomads working in coffee shops are slim, the risk is not zero. A disgruntled landlord, a jealous local, or a random spot check could lead to awkward questions. The consequences can range from a simple warning to deportation, fines, and a multi-year ban on re-entering not just that country, but potentially the entire Schengen Area in Europe. It is a high-stakes gamble, and not a viable strategy for a secure, long-term lifestyle.

Recognizing the economic benefit of attracting high-earning, location-independent professionals who spend money locally without taking local jobs, a paradigm shift has begun. Governments are starting to create a new, official channel. This is the rise of the digital nomad visa, a specific, long-term residence permit created for remote workers. As of 2025, more than fifty countries have launched or are in the process of launching such a program, a number that is growing every year. These visas are a game-changer, transforming the nomad from a quasi-legal tourist into a legally recognized temporary resident.

While the specifics vary from country to country, most digital nomad visas share a core set of requirements. The applicant must prove they are employed by a foreign company or are self-employed with foreign clients. Crucially, they must meet a minimum income threshold, demonstrating that they can support themselves without straining the local economy. For example, to qualify for Portugal's popular D8 Digital Nomad Visa, an applicant must show a consistent monthly income of at least four times the Portuguese minimum wage, which is roughly €3,480 per month. Spain requires a monthly income of around €2,760, while Croatia's is a more accessible €2,540.

Beyond income, you will almost universally need to provide proof of comprehensive health insurance that is valid in the host country, a clean criminal record certificate from your home country, and evidence that you have secured accommodation, at least for your initial period of stay. The application process is not trivial; it requires meticulous document gathering and often a visit to the host country's consulate in your home country. However, the reward is significant: the right to live and work legally for a year or more, with many of these visas offering a pathway to renewal and even permanent residency after several years. Countries from Europe like Greece and Italy to destinations in Asia like Japan, Thailand, and South Korea, and Latin America such as Costa Rica and Colombia have all entered this space, each offering a unique proposition for the global remote worker.

Digital nomad visas are not the only legal route. For decades before the term "digital nomad" was coined, people have been finding ways to live and work abroad. These alternative pathways are often more complex but can provide an even more stable long-term solution. For the freelancer or entrepreneur, a self-employment visa can be an excellent option. Germany, for instance, offers a well-regarded "Freiberufler" (freelance) visa. This requires more than just proof of income; you must submit a business plan, letters of intent from potential German clients, and prove that your work will have a positive impact on the local economy. While the bar is higher, it grants you the right to fully participate in the German economy and can lead to permanent residency.

For those with significant savings or passive income streams (such as from investments or rental properties), a "non-lucrative" or passive income visa can be the perfect fit. Spain's Non-Lucrative Visa is a popular example, designed for individuals who can support themselves without working. The financial requirement is substantial; for 2025, a single applicant must prove an annual income of at least €28,800, with an additional €7,200 for each dependent family member. This visa explicitly forbids you from working for a Spanish company, but it is often considered a legally sound option for remote workers whose income is generated entirely outside of Spain.

For younger nomads, typically those under 30 or 35, the Working Holiday Visa (WHV) presents a fantastic opportunity. These are reciprocal agreements between countries that allow young citizens to travel and work for up to a year. For US citizens, the options include countries like Australia, New Zealand, Ireland, and South Korea. While these visas are intended to allow you to take on local short-term jobs to fund your travels, they also provide a clear legal right to be in the country and work, which can comfortably cover your remote work activities. The requirements often include being a student or recent graduate and having sufficient funds for a return ticket.

Regardless of which visa you pursue, the application process itself is a lesson in patience and organization. It is not a task to be started a few weeks before your desired departure date; you should begin your research and document gathering at least six months in advance. The first step is always to find the official website of the embassy or consulate of the country you are applying to, in your country of residence. This is the only source of truth. Information on blogs and forums, while helpful, can be outdated.

You will need to gather a mountain of paperwork. This typically includes a valid passport with at least six months of validity remaining, passport-sized photos meeting specific dimensions, detailed bank statements, your employment or freelance contracts, and proof of health insurance. Many documents, such as your birth certificate or criminal record check, may need an "apostille," which is a form of international certification. Documents not in the local language will almost certainly require a certified translation. Keep both digital and multiple physical copies of everything. The process will likely culminate in an in-person appointment at the consulate, where you will submit your documents and answer questions about your intentions. After that, you wait. The processing time can take anywhere from a few weeks to several months.

Some nomads try to circumvent these lengthy processes by engaging in "visa runs." This involves staying in a country for the maximum visa-free period (often 90 days), crossing a border into a neighboring country for a day or two, and then re-entering to get a fresh 90-day stamp. This practice, while once common, is now viewed with increasing suspicion by immigration authorities. Border officials have the right to deny you re-entry if they believe you are attempting to live in the country rather than being a genuine tourist. Multiple entry and exit stamps in quick succession are a major red flag. A visa run should be seen not as a sustainable strategy, but as a temporary fix at best, and a sign that it is time to pursue a proper long-term visa.

Securing a visa is not the end of your legal obligations. Once you arrive in your new host country with your long-stay permit, you will often be required to complete several more steps. This can include registering your address with the local town hall or police station and applying for a formal residency card (a process that might involve another appointment and providing fingerprints). This residency card then becomes your primary form of identification in the country. It is also crucial to understand the rules for renewing your visa. This often requires proving you have spent a minimum amount of time in the country (typically more than six months per year) and continue to meet all the original requirements, like income and health insurance.

Navigating the world of visas and legalities is undoubtedly the most challenging administrative aspect of the digital nomad lifestyle. It demands research, preparation, and a commitment to doing things the right way. But the payoff is immense. A legal residency permit removes the constant background anxiety of being in a legal gray area. It opens doors to more integrated local experiences, like opening a local bank account or signing a long-term lease. Most importantly, it provides a stable, secure foundation upon which you can build not just a year of travel, but a truly sustainable life of freedom and flexibility anywhere in the world.

CHAPTER ELEVEN: The Art of Packing: How to Live Out of a Suitcase

The romantic image of the digital nomad often involves little more than a laptop and a passport, a symbol of ultimate freedom from material possessions. The reality, however, is that while you are freeing yourself from a fixed address, you are not freeing yourself from the need to have socks. Or a toothbrush. Or that specific charger without which your entire mobile office ceases to exist. This brings us to the surprisingly complex and deeply personal art of packing, an act that for a nomad is not a prelude to a vacation, but a fundamental curation of their entire life.

Learning to live out of a suitcase is a profound psychological shift. You are moving from a mindset of accumulation, where your home acts as a repository for everything you might someday need, to a mindset of intentionality, where every single object you possess must justify its existence through its utility, versatility, and weight. This is not about deprivation; it is about optimization. A well-packed bag is a masterpiece of personal engineering, a self-contained life-support system that provides comfort, efficiency, and peace of mind. Getting it right is a process of trial, error, and ruthless honesty. Getting it wrong means hauling a collection of useless, heavy objects across the globe, a constant and literal burden on your journey.

The first decision, and the one that will dictate every choice that follows, is your luggage. This is your mobile home, your shell. The debate between a backpack and a roller suitcase is a classic in travel circles, and for a digital nomad, the stakes are even higher. There is no single correct answer, only the answer that is correct for your travel style and physical comfort.

The travel backpack is the iconic choice for the adventurous nomad. Its primary advantage is mobility. When you arrive in a city of ancient cobblestones, crowded subways, and fourth-floor walk-up apartments, a backpack is your best friend. It keeps your hands free to navigate your phone, hold a ticket, or grab a coffee. It becomes an extension of your body, allowing you to move with an agility that a wheeled suitcase simply cannot match. However, that agility comes at a cost. Even the most ergonomic backpack becomes a heavy burden during a long walk from the bus station, and showing up to a client meeting with a giant hiking pack can feel less than professional.

The roller suitcase, on the other hand, offers a different kind of freedom: freedom for your back. Gliding a well-balanced suitcase through a smooth airport terminal is an effortless experience. Roller bags, particularly hard-shell models, also provide superior protection for your fragile electronics. They tend to be easier to organize, with clamshell designs that allow you to see all your belongings at once, rather than digging into the dark cavern of a top-loading backpack. The downside, of course, is that the moment you encounter a staircase, a gravel path, or a broken sidewalk, your elegant suitcase becomes a clumsy, awkward boulder that you have to drag behind you.

In recent years, a third option has emerged: the hybrid wheeled backpack. These bags attempt to offer the best of both worlds, with a set of wheels and a retractable handle for smooth surfaces, and a stowable harness system for when the terrain gets rough. While this sounds like the perfect solution, it is a compromise. The hardware for the wheels and handle adds significant weight and takes up valuable packing space, making them heavier and less spacious than their specialized counterparts.

Ultimately, the choice comes down to a realistic assessment of your travel style. If you envision yourself hopping between budget airlines and hostels in Southeast Asia, a backpack is likely the superior choice. If your nomadic life will be centered around long stays in modern European cities with excellent infrastructure, the convenience of a roller suitcase might win out. Whichever you choose, the next critical decision is size. The most liberating step a new nomad can take is to commit to traveling carry-on only.

The benefits of forgoing a checked bag are immense. First, you will save a significant amount of money on budget airline baggage fees. Second, you eliminate the risk of the airline losing your luggage, a disaster that can derail the start of your life in a new country. Third, you gain priceless time and agility. While others are crowded around the baggage carousel, you are already in a taxi on your way to your new apartment. This forces a discipline that is central to the art of packing. A 40-liter bag, the maximum size for most international carry-on, is all the space you have. This constraint is not a limitation; it is a clarification. It forces you to be ruthless, to pack only the essential, and to master the techniques of optimization.

Complementing your main bag is your personal item or daypack. This smaller bag is just as important as your primary luggage. It is what you will carry with you every day, containing your laptop, chargers, a water bottle, and other daily essentials. It also serves as your "in-flight bag," holding everything you need during travel. A good daypack should be comfortable, well-organized, and ideally, have a "pass-through" strap on the back that allows it to slide securely over the handle of your roller suitcase. The synergy between your main bag and your daypack is the foundation of your entire mobile ecosystem.

With your luggage selected, you face the main event: your wardrobe. This is where most aspiring nomads falter, falling into the trap of packing for every conceivable social and meteorological possibility. The key to avoiding this is to stop thinking of your clothes as individual items and start thinking of them as components in a system. This is the philosophy of the capsule wardrobe: a small, curated collection of versatile, high-quality pieces that can be mixed and matched to create a surprisingly large number of outfits.

The foundation of a successful capsule wardrobe is a strict color palette. Choose two or three neutral base colors that work well together, such as black, navy, grey, or tan. These will form the core of your wardrobe—your pants, jackets, and perhaps a few base-layer shirts. Then, add one or two accent colors that complement your base. These will be your T-shirts, scarves, or other accessories that add a touch of personality. By sticking to a predefined palette, you guarantee that almost every top you pack will match every bottom, maximizing your outfit combinations.

The second principle is layering. A well-designed layering system is far more effective and space-efficient than packing bulky, single-purpose items. Instead of a heavy winter coat, pack a system: a base layer (like a T-shirt), a mid-layer (like a long-sleeved merino wool shirt or a lightweight fleece), and an outer layer (a thin, waterproof, and windproof shell jacket). These three pieces can be worn individually in mild weather or combined to provide significant warmth and protection in colder, wetter climates, all while taking up a fraction of the space of a traditional coat.

Fabric choice is the secret weapon of the expert packer. Your goal is to choose materials that are lightweight, wrinkle-resistant, quick-drying, and versatile. At the top of this list is merino wool. This natural fiber is a miracle fabric for travelers: it regulates body temperature (keeping you cool in the heat and warm in the cold), wicks moisture away from your skin, and is naturally antimicrobial, meaning you can wear it multiple times without it smelling. A few merino wool T-shirts and a long-sleeved base layer are one of the best investments a nomad can make.

For other items, look to modern synthetic performance fabrics often found in athletic or outdoor clothing. These materials are designed to be durable, to dry in a matter of hours after being washed in a sink, and to resist wrinkling when stuffed into a bag. The one fabric to avoid at all costs is cotton. While comfortable, it is heavy, absorbs moisture, takes an eternity to dry, and wrinkles easily. A pair of cotton jeans can take up as much space and weight as three pairs of travel pants made from a technical fabric.

When deciding on quantity, a useful guideline is the "Rule of Three." For core items like shirts, underwear, and socks, pack three sets. You have one to wear, one in the wash, and one that is clean and ready to go. This system allows you to do small loads of laundry frequently, often in your apartment sink, rather than needing to find a laundromat constantly. For larger items like pants or shorts, two or three pairs are usually sufficient.

Footwear is often the heaviest and most awkward category to pack, so it is vital to choose wisely. Versatility is the ultimate goal. You need shoes that can handle a full day of walking on city streets, but that also look presentable enough for a nice dinner. A pair of stylish, all-black leather sneakers or comfortable walking shoes from a brand known for both form and function is often the perfect workhorse. Beyond this main pair, add a pair of lightweight sandals or flip-flops for warm weather and hostel showers. Depending on your lifestyle and planned activities, a third pair might be necessary, such as a pair of trail runners for hiking or a more formal pair of flats or boots. Always wear your heaviest, bulkiest pair of shoes on the plane to save space and weight in your bag.

Once you have selected your items, the next step is getting them into the bag. The most efficient method is to use packing cubes. These zippered fabric containers are the single greatest organizational tool for a traveler. They allow you to compartmentalize your clothing (e.g., one cube for tops, one for bottoms, one for underwear) and to compress them, squeezing out excess air to save a surprising amount of space. They transform the chaos of a stuffed suitcase into a neat, modular system, making it easy to find what you need without unpacking your entire bag.

Within the cubes, rolling your clothes is generally more space-efficient than folding and helps to minimize hard creases. For items like jackets or dress shirts, a neat fold may be better, but for T-shirts, pants, and sweaters, a tight roll is the way to go. Maximize every square inch of space. Stuff socks, underwear, or small electronic items inside your shoes. Utilize the small nooks and crannies that form around the edges of your packing cubes.

Your toiletries, or "liquids bag," demand similar downsizing. The global standard for carry-on liquids is that they must be in containers of 100ml (3.4 ounces) or less, and all containers must fit within a single, clear, one-liter bag. The easiest way to deal with this is to eliminate liquids wherever possible. The rise of solid toiletries has been a revolution for travelers. You can now find high-quality shampoo bars, conditioner bars, solid perfumes, and even toothpaste tablets that work just as well as their liquid counterparts, saving you space and hassle.

For any liquids that remain, invest in a set of high-quality, refillable silicone travel bottles. Don't rely on the free samples you have collected; they are prone to leaking. Build a minimalist first-aid kit containing the basics: painkillers, assorted bandages, antiseptic wipes, blister treatment, and any personal prescription medications. Remember to carry a copy of your prescription, and keep all medications in their original packaging to avoid issues at security or customs. And for everything else, from sunscreen to contact lens solution, embrace the "buy it there" philosophy. Unless you are heading to a remote jungle outpost, you can purchase most common toiletries anywhere in the world.

Beyond clothes and toiletries, there are a few miscellaneous items that consistently prove their worth. A quick-drying microfiber travel towel is much smaller and more absorbent than a traditional cotton towel. A universal travel adapter with multiple USB ports is an absolute necessity for keeping your devices charged. A portable power bank is a lifesaver on long travel days. A reusable water bottle is not only environmentally friendly but will save you a small fortune. A simple headlamp can be invaluable, whether you're navigating a poorly lit street at night or trying to find something in your bag in a dark hostel dorm without waking everyone up.

Once you think you have everything assembled, it is time for the final, crucial step: the shakedown. Lay every single item you plan to pack out on your floor or bed. Pick up each object and ask yourself a series of tough questions. Have I used this in the last three months? Do I have a definite, specific plan to use this on my trip? Does this item serve more than one purpose? If I don't bring it, can I buy it or borrow it there? Be ruthless. That "just in case" outfit is almost never worn. The pile of "maybe" books can be replaced with an e-reader.

A helpful mental filter is the 20/20 rule: if you can replace an item for under twenty dollars, in under twenty minutes from where you will be staying, you probably don't need to pack it. This applies to things like umbrellas, basic hats, or extra charging cables. Your goal is to eliminate every non-essential item. After you have purged the unnecessary, do a test pack. If you have to sit on your suitcase to get it to close, you still have too much stuff. Remove more.

It is vital to understand that your first packing list will not be perfect. You will inevitably bring things you never touch and find yourself desperately wishing for something you left behind. That is part of the process. Packing is not a one-time event but an evolving skill. After your first few months on the road, you will have a much clearer idea of what you truly need. Don't be afraid to adjust your kit. Mail non-essential items home. Donate the sweater you never wear. Buy the piece of gear you find yourself missing. The goal is to continuously refine your mobile life, stripping it down to a perfectly optimized collection of objects that serve and support your journey, rather than weigh it down.

CHAPTER TWELVE: Your Digital Toolkit: Essential Apps and Gear for a Mobile Office

Your new office has no walls, no water cooler, and no IT department to call when the Wi-Fi acts up. Your workspace is a fluid concept, a collection of pixels and circuits that you carry on your back. This chapter is about the tools of the trade. The success of your mobile professional life depends not just on your skills, but on the reliability and efficiency of the gear and software you use every day. Assembling your digital toolkit is an act of meticulous curation, a balance of power, portability, and resilience.

Think of it as building a self-sufficient spaceship. Every component must be carefully chosen for its function and its weight, because you are the one who has to carry it. The goal is to create a seamless, professional, and secure work environment that can be deployed in minutes, whether you are in a bustling airport lounge, a quiet library, or a beachfront café. This isn't about having the most expensive or flashiest gadgets; it's about having the right tools that work for you, tools that fade into the background and let you focus on what actually matters: doing great work.

The heart of your mobile office, the single most important piece of hardware you will own, is your laptop. It is your connection to your clients, your primary means of production, and your entertainment center. Choosing the right one is a decision that will impact your daily productivity and your physical comfort. The perfect nomad laptop is a master of compromise, excelling in four key areas: portability, power, battery life, and durability.

Portability is the most obvious factor. Every gram matters when you are living out of a suitcase. You are looking for a machine that is both thin and light, ideally weighing under 1.5 kilograms (about 3.3 pounds). Screen size is a personal preference, but the 13-to-14-inch range is often the sweet spot, providing enough screen real estate to work comfortably without becoming cumbersome to pack and carry.

Power is about matching the machine to your work. A freelance writer who lives in Google Docs has vastly different needs than a video editor who works with 4K footage. Be honest about your typical workload. For most tasks like writing, marketing, and web development, a modern processor with at least 16GB of RAM is more than sufficient. If your work involves graphic design, video editing, or programming, you will need to invest in a more powerful CPU, a dedicated graphics card, and potentially more RAM. Underpowered hardware is a constant source of frustration and a bottleneck to your productivity.

Battery life is the metric of true freedom. Your ability to work is directly tied to your proximity to a power outlet. A laptop with a mediocre battery tethers you to the wall, limiting your choice of workspaces. Your goal should be a machine that can comfortably last a full workday of mixed use—at least eight to ten hours of real-world screen-on time. This allows you to spend a full day at a café without the anxiety of watching your battery percentage plummet. Always look at independent reviews for battery life benchmarks, as the manufacturer's claims are often wildly optimistic.

Finally, durability is the unsung hero of nomadic gear. Your laptop will be subjected to more stress than a typical office computer. It will be jostled in overhead bins, carried through dusty streets, and exposed to varying levels of humidity. Look for machines with a solid, well-built chassis, preferably made of aluminum or a high-quality alloy. Keyboards that are resistant to spills and robust hinges can mean the difference between a minor inconvenience and a major repair in a foreign country where service options may be limited.

With your hardware chosen, you need to consider the small army of peripherals that transform your laptop from a standalone device into a comfortable and functional workstation. The most important of these are your ergonomic tools. Hunching over a laptop screen for eight hours a day is a fast track to chronic neck and back pain. Investing in a portable ergonomic setup is not a luxury; it is a critical investment in your long-term health.

The core of this setup is a portable laptop stand. Devices like the Roost Laptop Stand or the Nexstand are incredibly lightweight, fold down to the size of a small umbrella, and elevate your screen to eye level. This simple change has a profound impact on your posture. Of course, with your screen elevated, you will need an external keyboard and mouse. Look for compact, wireless models that are easy to pack. A slim keyboard like the Logitech MX Keys Mini and a small, precise mouse like the Logitech MX Anywhere are popular choices that offer a full-sized typing and mousing experience in a travel-friendly package.

Power management is the next priority. A high-quality portable power bank is your lifeline on long travel days or in places with unreliable electricity. Look for a model with a high capacity (at least 20,000mAh) and, critically, a USB-C Power Delivery (PD) port capable of outputting enough wattage (typically 45W or more) to charge your laptop directly. This turns any seat into a potential workspace. Paired with this should be a single, high-quality universal travel adapter. Don't buy a cheap one at the airport. Invest in a reputable brand that has multiple USB ports, allowing you to charge your laptop, phone, and power bank simultaneously from a single outlet.

Audio and video quality can make or break your professional image. The built-in microphones and webcams on most laptops are notoriously poor. A pair of high-quality, noise-canceling headphones is one of the best investments a nomad can make. They create a bubble of silence in a noisy café, allow you to take professional-sounding calls, and make long flights infinitely more pleasant. Whether you prefer the deep immersion of over-ear models like the Sony WH-1000XM series or the portability of in-ear buds, this is an essential tool for focus.

For your video calls, an external webcam will make you look dramatically more professional than the grainy, poorly lit image from your laptop's built-in camera. A simple, portable 1080p webcam that can clip onto the top of your screen shows clients that you take your remote work setup seriously.

Finally, you need a bulletproof data backup strategy. The "3-2-1 Rule" is the gold standard: keep at least three copies of your data, on two different types of media, with one copy stored off-site. For a nomad, this translates to a simple system. Your primary copy lives on your laptop's internal drive. Your secondary copy is an automatic, continuous backup to a cloud storage service like Google Drive, Dropbox, or iCloud. This is your off-site copy. Your third copy, the one that can save you if your laptop is stolen and the internet is down, should be a periodic backup to a small, portable solid-state drive (SSD). These drives are incredibly fast, durable, and small enough to be kept in a separate bag from your laptop.

With your hardware in place, it is time to load it with the software that will power your productivity. Your software suite is the invisible framework of your mobile office, enabling you to communicate, collaborate, and create from anywhere.

At the core of any remote operation is the communication hub. For team-based work, this is almost always a combination of Slack for asynchronous text-based communication and Zoom or Google Meet for real-time video conferencing. Mastering the etiquette and features of these platforms is fundamental to being an effective remote collaborator.

To keep your work organized, a project management tool is essential. For freelancers and solo operators, a tool like Trello, with its simple, card-based "kanban" system, can be perfect for tracking projects through different stages. For those working in teams, Asana provides a more robust platform for assigning tasks, setting deadlines, and tracking progress. A newer category of "all-in-one" workspace apps, with Notion being the most prominent example, can serve as your project manager, note-taking app, and personal wiki—a digital "second brain" for organizing both your work and your life.

Your creation tools will depend on your profession, but the trend is overwhelmingly towards cloud-based platforms. Google Workspace (Docs, Sheets, Slides) and Microsoft 365 have made it possible to create, edit, and collaborate on documents, spreadsheets, and presentations in real-time from any device with a web browser. The days of being tied to a single machine with locally installed software are largely over.

To protect your most valuable asset—your focus—consider using specialized productivity apps. The Pomodoro Technique, which involves working in focused 25-minute intervals with short breaks, can be managed with a simple timer or a dedicated app like Forest, which gamifies the process. If you find yourself easily distracted by social media or news sites, a website blocker like Freedom can be a powerful tool for enforcing deep work sessions. For freelancers who bill by the hour, a time-tracking app like Toggl or Harvest is indispensable for creating accurate invoices and understanding how you are spending your time.

This entire ecosystem of hardware and software is built on a foundation of internet connectivity, and much of that will happen over public Wi-Fi networks in cafes, airports, and co-working spaces. This convenience comes with a major security risk. Public networks are notoriously insecure, making it easy for malicious actors to snoop on your activity and intercept sensitive data like passwords or financial information. This is why your digital defense kit is not optional; it is a fundamental part of your professional setup.

The single most important security tool you will use is a Virtual Private Network, or VPN. A VPN creates a secure, encrypted tunnel between your device and the internet, making your connection private and shielding your data from anyone else on the network. It also allows you to route your traffic through a server in another country, which can be useful for accessing services or websites that are geo-restricted. You must use a reputable, paid VPN service; "free" VPNs often have questionable privacy practices and may sell your data to make money.

Your second line of defense is a password manager. In the modern digital world, you have dozens, if not hundreds, of online accounts. Using the same simple password for all of them is a catastrophic security risk. A password manager, such as 1Password or Bitwarden, solves this problem. It generates and stores long, complex, unique passwords for every site you use, and you only have to remember a single master password to access your vault. It is the key to effortless, ironclad password security.

You must pair this with Two-Factor Authentication (2FA) wherever it is offered. As mentioned before, you should always opt for an app-based authenticator like Google Authenticator or Authy over SMS-based codes. These apps generate time-sensitive codes on your device, which are not vulnerable to SIM-swapping scams and work even when you don't have cellular service.

Finally, prepare for the worst-case scenario: a lost or stolen device. Ensure that your device's built-in tracking services, like Apple's "Find My" or Google's "Find My Device," are enabled. These allow you to locate, lock, or remotely erase your device if it goes missing. For an added layer of protection, a third-party service like Prey can provide more detailed tracking and even take pictures from the device's camera to help identify a thief.

While your laptop is your primary workstation, your smartphone is your pocket command center. It is your backup internet connection (via hotspot), your navigator, your translator, and your primary communication device. Keep it loaded with essential apps for life on the road: Google Maps (with downloaded offline maps for your current city), Google Translate (with offline language packs), WhatsApp for ubiquitous communication, your banking and budgeting apps, and a travel organization app like TripIt to keep all your booking confirmations in one place.

Assembling your digital toolkit is a process of continuous refinement. You will learn what works for you, what you can live without, and what new tool might make your life easier. But by starting with a solid foundation—a reliable laptop, an ergonomic setup, a smart software suite, and a robust security protocol—you create a mobile office that is not a source of stress, but a powerful engine for a life of freedom and productivity.

CHAPTER THIRTEEN: Choosing Your Destination: A World of Possibilities

The moment has arrived. You've cultivated the right mindset, secured a location-independent income, navigated the legalities, and mastered the art of fitting your life into a 40-liter bag. The theoretical has become tangible. Before you lies a world map, no longer a piece of classroom decor, but a menu of potential offices, homes, and adventures. This newfound freedom, however, presents a daunting challenge: the paradox of choice. When you can go anywhere, how do you decide where to begin? The sheer number of options can be paralyzing, leading many to simply default to the same handful of destinations they see on social media.

This chapter is designed to be your compass. Its purpose is to move you beyond the generic "Top 10" listicles and equip you with a practical framework for making a decision that is uniquely right for you. The perfect nomadic destination is not a universal constant; it is a deeply personal alignment of your professional requirements, financial realities, and lifestyle aspirations. What is paradise for a freelance developer who loves surfing might be a logistical nightmare for a remote employee who needs to be on New York time. Our goal is to dissect the key criteria that matter, empowering you to create a personalized shortlist of places where you won't just visit, but truly thrive.

The Foundational Trio: The Non-Negotiables

Before you even begin to dream of mountain vistas or ancient city streets, you must filter your options through a pragmatic lens of three non-negotiable pillars. These are the logistical bedrock upon which any successful nomadic experience is built. A failure in any one of these areas can turn a dream destination into a source of constant frustration.

The first and most sacred of these pillars is internet reliability. This is the digital oxygen you need to survive. Without a stable, fast connection, your professional life grinds to a halt. It's not enough for a country to have "good internet" on paper; you need to know about the reality on the ground. Advertised speeds mean little if the connection drops every thirty minutes. Your research here must be granular. Use resources like Nomad List which crowdsources internet speed data from users in thousands of cities. However, don't stop there. Dive into local expat and digital nomad Facebook groups and ask specific, recent questions: "How is the Wi-Fi in the El Poblado neighborhood of Medellín right now?" or "Can anyone recommend a co-working space in Lisbon with a reliable fiber connection for video calls?".

Your second pillar is the cost of living. This is where you put the principle of geoarbitrage, discussed in Chapter Eight, into practice. Your financial freedom is directly tied to the delta between your earnings and your expenses. A lower cost of living can dramatically accelerate your savings goals, reduce your work stress, and improve your overall quality of life. Websites like Numbeo provide detailed, user-submitted data on the cost of everything from a liter of milk to a one-bedroom apartment in the city center. This allows you to build a sample budget and realistically assess the financial viability of a location. A monthly budget of $2,000 might be a struggle in a city like Barcelona, but could afford you a life of considerable comfort in a place like Chiang Mai or Buenos Aires.

The final pillar of the foundational trio is safety and stability. Your personal safety is paramount, and your definition of it must be comprehensive. It extends beyond low crime rates to include political stability, the quality of local infrastructure like power and water, and the general ease of navigating daily life. Begin your research with your home country's government travel advisories, which provide a baseline understanding of any significant risks. Then, seek out nuanced, on-the-ground perspectives. Read blogs and watch videos from nomads who have recently spent time in your potential destinations. Pay special attention to advice from travelers who share your demographic, as the experience of a solo female traveler can be very different from that of a male couple.

The Professional Filters: Aligning with Your Work Life

With the foundational requirements met, the next layer of your decision-making process should focus on the specific needs of your professional life. A destination must not only be livable but also conducive to your productivity and career growth.

The most critical professional filter is time zone compatibility. For freelancers with asynchronous workflows, this may be less of a concern. For a remote employee who is required to be online for team meetings during specific business hours, it is a make-or-break factor. A twelve-hour time difference can force you into a nocturnal work schedule that is draining and unsustainable. Look at a world map and identify the broad time zone "bands" that are compatible with your work. If your team is in California, living in Latin America is a seamless experience. If you try to do the same job from Southeast Asia, you will be starting your workday when your colleagues are ending theirs.

Next, consider your ideal work environment. Are you the kind of person who can focus for eight hours a day in your apartment, or do you need the structure and social buzz of a dedicated workspace? The availability and quality of co-working spaces and a laptop-friendly café culture can dramatically impact your daily happiness and productivity. A quick search on Google Maps can reveal the number of co-working spaces in a city, but you'll need to dig deeper into their websites and reviews to understand their vibe, amenities, and cost. Some cities, like Lisbon and Bangkok, have a rich and diverse co-working scene, while in others it may be a nascent concept.

Finally, a brief but crucial callback to Chapter Ten: the visa situation. A city is only a viable option if you can legally reside there. This must be a primary filter in your search. Does the country offer a digital nomad visa? If so, do you meet the income requirements? For instance, Portugal's popular visa requires a monthly income of around €3,480, while Spain's is approximately €2,760 and Croatia's is about €3,295. If you are planning a shorter stay on a tourist entry, how long can you legally remain? Be aware of regional agreements like the Schengen Area in Europe, where your time is cumulative across all member countries. Your legal right to be in a country should be a black-and-white consideration that helps you narrow down your list from the very beginning.

The Personal Filters: Crafting Your Desired Lifestyle

This is where the process becomes truly personal. With the practicalities sorted, you can now focus on the elements that will bring you joy and fulfillment. This is about matching a destination's character to your own.

Start by considering the pace of life and city size. Are you energized by the chaotic, 24/7 thrum of a megacity like Mexico City or Tokyo? Or does your soul crave the more relaxed, manageable pace of a smaller city like Da Nang in Vietnam or the surf town of Canggu in Bali? Be honest with yourself about the kind of environment that allows you to feel both stimulated and at ease. There is no right answer, only the answer that is right for you.

Climate and environment play a huge role in your day-to-day experience. The dream of an "endless summer" is a powerful motivator for many, but it is not a universal desire. Do you want to surf in the morning before work? Then a coastal town is a must. Do you live for mountain hiking on the weekends? Look for cities nestled in dramatic landscapes. Or are you a culture-vulture who wants world-class museums and theaters at your doorstep? Your hobbies and passions are a powerful guide to finding a place that will feel like more than just a temporary office.

Think about your desire for cultural immersion. How important is it for you to be in a place where English is widely spoken? Operating in a "bubble" where you can easily get by in English offers a lower-friction experience, especially for new nomads. However, grappling with a new language and culture, while challenging, can be one of the most rewarding aspects of this lifestyle. Your preference on this spectrum will guide you towards either established expat hubs or destinations further off the beaten path.

Finally, while we will explore this in depth in Chapter Sixteen, consider the social scene. Research the type of community that exists in a potential destination. Is it known for a large, transient population of young nomads, a more settled community of long-term expatriates, or is it a place where your social life will be built primarily around local connections? Browsing through local Meetup groups and city-specific nomad forums can give you a feel for the social fabric of a place before you ever step on a plane.

Putting It All Together: From Long List to Short List

With these filters in mind, the process of choosing becomes a manageable exercise rather than an overwhelming guess. A practical method is to create a simple spreadsheet. List your top ten or fifteen potential destinations in the first column. In the subsequent columns, list the criteria that matter most to you: cost of living, internet speed, time zone, climate, co-working availability, and so on. Rate each city on a scale of one to five for each criterion. This simple act of quantification can bring surprising clarity, revealing which locations truly align with your priorities.

Remember that you do not have to find the one perfect city and commit to it for a year. A highly effective strategy, especially for your first year, is the "hub and spoke" model. Choose a major, well-connected city that scores highly on your list—like Lisbon, Bangkok, or Mexico City—and use it as a stable base for three to six months. From this "hub," you can take shorter, two-to-three-week "spoke" trips to explore nearby cities and countries, gathering real-world data without the hassle of moving all your belongings each time.

A final word on the well-trodden path. Cities like Chiang Mai, Bali, Lisbon, and Medellín are popular for a reason. They offer a proven combination of affordability, good infrastructure, and a ready-made community. For a first-time nomad, starting in one of these "hotspots" can be a fantastic way to ease into the lifestyle and build your confidence. The downside is that they can sometimes feel crowded or less than authentic. Don't be afraid to use these hubs as a launchpad, a place to find your footing before venturing out to a destination that is uniquely yours. The world is a vast and varied menu; your task is simply to find the dish that best suits your palate.

CHAPTER FOURTEEN: Finding a Place to Live: From Co-living Spaces to Short-Term Rentals

You've done the research. The pins on your world map have been narrowed down to a single, exciting city. Your flight is booked, your visa is in order, and your financial runway is paved. Now, you face the most immediate and tangible of all nomadic challenges: finding a place to put your suitcase down. This is about more than just a roof over your head. Your choice of accommodation is the single biggest factor in your monthly budget, and it will profoundly shape your daily experience, impacting your productivity, your social life, and your overall sense of well-being in a new place.

The search for a temporary home is a very different beast from traditional apartment hunting. You are not signing a twelve-month lease or applying for a mortgage. You are looking for a flexible, furnished, and functional base of operations that you can secure with minimal friction. The market has evolved to meet this demand, and today's nomad has a rich menu of options, from hyper-social co-living communities to private, quiet apartments. This chapter is your guide to navigating this menu, helping you to find the right space for your budget, your work style, and your personal needs.

The most critical piece of advice, the golden rule of nomadic housing, is this: never, ever book a long-term rental sight unseen. The photographs may be professionally staged, the description may be glowing, but you cannot know the reality of a place until you are standing in it. You cannot know that the "charming, vibrant street" is actually a 24-hour party zone, that the "cozy" apartment has no natural light, or that the promised high-speed Wi-Fi is shared with twelve other units and slows to a crawl every afternoon.

To avoid this costly mistake, you must adopt the "landing pad" strategy. Your goal for your first few days or your first week in a new city is not to find your perfect home, but to secure a safe, comfortable, and centrally located base from which you can conduct your real housing search. This temporary base allows you to get over your jet lag, explore different neighborhoods in person, and view potential longer-term options with your own eyes. It transforms a stressful, high-stakes decision into a more relaxed and informed process.

For this initial landing pad, you have several excellent options. Hostels are the classic choice for the budget-conscious traveler. They offer an unbeatable combination of low cost and social opportunities, making it easy to meet other travelers and get on-the-ground tips. The modern hostel scene has evolved far beyond crowded dorm rooms; many now offer private rooms with en-suite bathrooms, providing a dose of privacy while still giving you access to the communal kitchen and social areas. They are a fantastic way to get the lay of the land for a few days.

If your budget allows for a bit more comfort and privacy, a hotel or an aparthotel can be a great choice. The reliability is a major plus; you know you will have a clean room, a comfortable bed, and professional staff to assist you. Aparthotels are a particularly good option as they often include a small kitchenette, allowing you to prepare simple meals and save on the cost of eating out three times a day. While hotels can feel isolating and are too expensive for a long-term stay, they provide a frictionless and comfortable environment for your first few nights.

A short booking of a few days on a platform like Airbnb or Booking.com can also serve as an excellent landing pad. This gives you a taste of apartment life from the very beginning. The key is to book a room in a shared apartment or a small studio in a neighborhood you are already considering for a longer stay. This is a low-commitment way to test-drive a specific area of the city. During this initial period, your mission is reconnaissance. Walk everywhere. Get a feel for the rhythm of different neighborhoods.

Visit the local grocery stores, cafés, and parks. You are not just looking for an apartment; you are looking for your new life.

Once you have your feet on the ground, you can begin the search for your home for the next month, or three, or six. For the vast majority of digital nomads, this means diving into the world of furnished, short-term rentals. This is where you will find the sweet spot of comfort, convenience, and flexibility.

The undisputed giants in this space are platforms like Airbnb, VRBO, and other regional equivalents. While these sites are famous for short vacation stays, they have become a primary tool for nomads seeking monthly rentals. The secret is to always search for a stay of at least 28 days. This will automatically trigger significant monthly discounts, which can often be as much as 40-60% off the nightly rate. This simple change in your search parameters transforms the platform from an expensive vacation tool into a viable housing solution.

When vetting a listing on these platforms, you need to become a detective. The reviews are your most valuable source of intelligence. Do not just look at the star rating; read the last six months of reviews in detail. Look for recurring themes. If multiple people mention that the Wi-Fi is unreliable or the street is noisy, believe them. Pay close attention to reviews from other long-term guests, as their experience will be the most relevant to yours.

The photographs are your next clue. Look for clear, well-lit photos of every room. Be wary of listings that only show you close-ups of decorative pillows and artfully arranged fruit bowls. You need to see the practicalities. Is there a proper desk and chair, or will you be working from the couch? Does the kitchen look well-equipped, or is it just a microwave and a hot plate? A very powerful pro-tip is to message the host before booking and ask for a screenshot of a recent internet speed test (from a site like Speedtest.net). A host who is happy to provide this is a host who is confident in their connection. One who evades the question is a major red flag.

For those who crave community and a built-in social life, the rise of co-living spaces has been a revelation. A co-living arrangement typically involves a private, fully furnished bedroom and bathroom, combined with extensive, high-quality shared spaces. These often include a large communal kitchen, a comfortable lounge area, a movie room, a gym, and, most importantly, a dedicated co-working space with business-grade internet.

The advantages of co-living are immense, especially for a solo nomad arriving in a new city. It provides an instant community. The social friction of meeting new people is removed, as you are living with a group of like-minded professionals from around the world. These spaces almost always organize regular community events, from group dinners and workshops to weekend excursions. It is a powerful antidote to the loneliness that can sometimes accompany a nomadic life.

The convenience is also a major selling point. Everything is included in a single monthly bill: your rent, all utilities, high-speed Wi-Fi, and often weekly cleaning of your room and the common areas. There are no surprise electricity bills or the hassle of setting up an internet contract. You simply arrive, unpack, and are ready to live and work from day one. Websites like Coliving.com, Kndrd, and Anyplace are excellent resources for finding and comparing co-living options globally. The primary downside is cost; co-living is often more expensive than renting a private studio apartment. You are paying a premium for the convenience, community, and amenities.

For nomads planning a longer stay of six months or more, and for those on a tighter budget, the most cost-effective option is to tap into the local rental market directly. This is the path to the best deals and the most authentic living experience, but it is also the one fraught with the most challenges. This involves using local real estate websites—like Idealista in Spain, Fotocasa in Portugal, or Immobilienscout24 in Germany—or joining local housing groups on Facebook.

The first major hurdle is often the language barrier. Listings, communication with landlords, and lease agreements will almost always be in the local language. You will need to be comfortable using translation tools or, ideally, have a local friend who can help you. The second challenge is the bureaucracy. Local rentals typically require a formal lease, a significant security deposit (often one to three months' rent), and sometimes even proof of a local bank account or a local guarantor.

This is a strategy best undertaken once you are already on the ground. It is nearly impossible to secure a good local rental from abroad. Landlords will want to meet you in person, and you will absolutely want to see the apartment before committing to a multi-month lease and handing over a large deposit. While this path requires more effort, the reward can be substantial savings and a deeper integration into the local community.

Beyond these primary options, there are alternative strategies for the more adventurous or flexible nomad. House sitting has emerged as a popular way to secure free accommodation. In exchange for looking after someone's home and, most commonly, their pets while they are on vacation, you get to live in a comfortable, fully-equipped home for free. This is an incredible value exchange, offering a deeply local experience. The key is responsibility; you are not just a guest, you are a caretaker. Platforms like TrustedHousesitters are the market leaders, connecting homeowners with sitters around the world. The platform has a subscription fee, and the competition for desirable sits in popular locations can be intense.

Once you have identified a promising option, it is time to perform your due diligence. Do not be afraid to ask the host or manager a detailed list of questions before you commit. Your work depends on the answers. Beyond the internet speed test, ask about the workspace setup, the noise levels from neighbors and the street, and exactly what is included in the rent.

Use technology to your advantage. Once you have a specific address, use Google Street View to take a virtual walk around the neighborhood. Does it look safe and well-lit? What is the general vibe? Use Google Maps to check the proximity to essential amenities. How far is the nearest supermarket? Where is the closest gym or park? How convenient is public transportation? This virtual reconnaissance can save you from a major real-world mistake.

When it comes to booking and payment, especially with individuals rather than established companies, caution is key. For your first rental with a new host, always book through a reputable platform that offers payment protection, like Airbnb. Never, ever agree to pay a deposit or the first month's rent via a direct bank transfer or a service like Western Union before you have arrived and seen the property. Scams targeting eager renters are common, and once your money is sent via a direct transfer, it is gone forever.

Finally, once you have secured your spot and walked through the door, the last step is to make it your own. Living out of a suitcase does not mean you have to live in a sterile, impersonal environment. The simple act of fully unpacking your clothes into the closet, rather than living out of your bag, can have a profound psychological effect. It signals to your brain that you have arrived, that this is a place of stability, even if only for a month.

Bring a few small, lightweight items that make a space feel like yours. This could be a small travel candle with a familiar scent, a photo of loved ones, or a lightweight, portable Bluetooth speaker for playing your favorite music. Create a routine. Designate a specific, clutter-free area as your dedicated workspace. Find your local coffee shop. These small rituals are the building blocks of creating a sense of "home," a comfortable and productive base from which you can launch your daily work and your global adventures.

CHAPTER FIFTEEN: Staying Connected: Mastering Wi-Fi and International Communication

Connectivity is the invisible, non-negotiable lifeblood of the digital nomad. It is the vital utility that powers your business, bridges the distance to your loved ones, and transforms a foreign city into a functional workspace. The romantic image of working from a remote, off-grid cabin is a fantasy best reserved for a vacation; the professional reality is that your freedom is directly proportional to the strength of your signal. A slow, unreliable connection is more than just an annoyance; it is a direct threat to your income and your sanity.

Mastering the art of staying connected is not a matter of luck. It is a proactive, strategic skill, a combination of diligent research, clever redundancy, and the right combination of tools. The seasoned nomad does not simply show up in a new country and hope for the best. They arrive with a multi-layered plan, knowing how they will get online the moment they step off the plane, what their backup options are, and how they will manage the flow of communication between their new temporary home and the rest of the world. This chapter is your technical manual for building that plan, demystifying the world of Wi-Fi, SIM cards, and global communication so that your connection becomes a reliable asset, not a daily source of stress.

The Quest for Reliable Wi-Fi

The term "Wi-Fi" is a broad one, encompassing everything from a blazing-fast, business-grade fiber optic line to a sluggish, overburdened signal at a busy café. Your first task in any new location is to secure the best possible connection for your primary workspace. This is not the time for compromise. Think of your Wi-Fi options as a hierarchy, a pyramid of reliability where you should always aim for the top.

At the absolute pinnacle of this hierarchy is your own private, vetted connection in a medium- to long-term rental apartment. This is the gold standard. It provides the security, stability, and speed you need for high-stakes work like critical video conferences or large file transfers. The crucial word here, however, is "vetted." As we discussed in the previous chapter, you can never take an Airbnb host's claim of "fast Wi-Fi" at face value. Before you ever commit to a month-long stay, it is perfectly reasonable and highly recommended to ask for a screenshot of a recent internet speed test from a site like Speedtest.net or Fast.com.

Understanding the results of that test is a critical skill. It will show you three key numbers. Download speed, measured in megabits per second (Mbps), determines how quickly you can pull data from the internet, affecting things like streaming video or loading complex websites. For most remote work, anything above 25 Mbps is functional. Upload speed is your second metric, and for many nomads, it is even more important. This determines how quickly you can send data to the internet. A poor upload speed will result in a glitchy, pixelated video feed on your Zoom calls and make sending large files a painfully slow process. You should look for an absolute minimum of 5-10 Mbps for a smooth video conferencing experience. The final number is latency, or "ping," measured in milliseconds (ms). This is the reaction time of your connection. A low ping (under 50ms) is essential for clear, lag-free voice and video calls.

The next tier down, the silver standard, is a reputable co-working space. For nomads who thrive on a structured work environment or find their apartment connection to be lacking, a co-working membership can be a sound investment. These spaces are businesses built on the promise of productivity, and their primary selling point is business-grade, reliable internet. They often have redundant connections from multiple providers and backup power generators, meaning that even if the entire neighborhood has an outage, you can keep working. Before signing up for a monthly membership, almost all co-working spaces offer a free day pass, allowing you to test out the connection, the atmosphere, and the ergonomics of their chairs.

At the base of the pyramid is the bronze tier: the public Wi-Fi found in cafés, libraries, and hotel lobbies. This is the most romanticized version of the nomad office, but it is also the least reliable. While a café can be a wonderful place to work for a few hours on low-stakes tasks, you are at the mercy of a connection that is being shared by dozens of other people. It is generally not a suitable environment for an important client call. Furthermore, public Wi-Fi networks are inherently insecure, making the use of a VPN (as discussed in Chapter Twelve) an absolute necessity. Remember the etiquette of the café office: buy something every couple of hours, don't hog a large table during the lunch rush, and keep your calls quiet and brief.

Your strategy should not be to rely on a single point in this hierarchy, but to build redundancy. The ultimate safety net, the tool that frees you from the tyranny of the Wi-Fi signal, is your own personal hotspot. By enabling the hotspot feature on your smartphone, you can turn its mobile data connection into a private Wi-Fi network for your laptop. This is your get-out-of-jail-free card. When the power goes out at your apartment or the café Wi-Fi grinds to a halt right before a deadline, you can be back online in seconds. For nomads whose work is absolutely mission-critical, a dedicated mobile hotspot device (often called a MiFi) can be an even better solution, as it won't drain your phone's battery and often has more powerful antennas for a stronger signal.

Mastering Mobile Data on the Move

A personal hotspot is only as good as the mobile data plan that powers it. For the digital nomad, a smartphone without a data connection is little more than a pocket-sized camera. Navigating the world of international mobile data can seem complex, with a bewildering array of SIM cards, roaming plans, and new technologies. In reality, it boils down to a few key options, and the right strategy can provide you with fast, affordable data in almost every country on earth.

The first and most important prerequisite is ensuring your smartphone is "unlocked." This means it is not contractually tied to a single carrier and is free to accept a SIM card from any provider. If you bought your phone outright, it is likely already unlocked. If you purchased it as part of a multi-year contract, you may need to complete the contract or pay a fee to have your carrier unlock it. Verifying that your phone is unlocked before you leave your home country is one of the most critical pre-departure tasks.

With an unlocked phone in hand, your most cost-effective option for stays of a month or longer is to purchase a local prepaid SIM card upon arrival. This strategy allows you to tap into the local mobile infrastructure at local prices, which are often a fraction of what you would pay for international roaming. In many countries, you can buy a SIM card directly at the airport in the arrivals hall. While this is incredibly convenient, it can sometimes be slightly more expensive than buying one from an official provider's store in the city center. The registration process will almost always require your passport, and the vendor will usually help you with the activation. Topping up your data plan is typically a simple process, done via the provider's app, their website, or by purchasing scratch cards from one of the thousands of small convenience stores.

The modern, and increasingly popular, alternative to a physical SIM card is the eSIM. An eSIM is an embedded, digital SIM that is built into most newer smartphone models. It functions exactly like a physical SIM, but without the tiny piece of plastic. The advantages for a nomad are enormous. You can browse, purchase, and install a data plan for your destination country online before you even leave home. This means you are connected the moment your plane's wheels touch the tarmac. You can store multiple eSIM profiles on your phone at once, allowing you to switch between providers with a simple tap in your settings. Crucially, because the eSIM doesn't occupy your physical SIM tray, you can keep your home country's SIM card in your phone, ensuring you can still receive important calls or text messages to your regular number.

A host of global eSIM providers, such as Airalo, Holafly, and Nomad, have emerged to serve this market. They offer data plans for hundreds of countries, often with flexible durations, from a few days to a few months. While the per-gigabyte cost of an eSIM can sometimes be slightly higher than a local SIM, the convenience and flexibility are often worth the small premium. You avoid the hassle of finding a store, dealing with a potential language barrier, and fumbling with a tiny SIM card and an ejector tool.

The third option is to use an international roaming plan from your provider back home. Some carriers, like Google Fi or T-Mobile in the United States, have built their reputation on offering seamless, affordable data roaming in a huge number of countries. The primary benefit is absolute convenience; you do nothing, and your phone simply works when you arrive. However, for most other carriers, roaming is an incredibly expensive option, with exorbitant per-megabyte charges that can lead to a shocking bill. Another downside is that your data speeds can sometimes be throttled or "deprioritized" compared to local customers. International roaming is best viewed as an excellent temporary solution for your first 24 hours in a country or for very short trips, rather than a sustainable long-term strategy.

The optimal strategy is often a hybrid approach. Purchase a small eSIM data package for your destination before you depart. This gives you the peace of mind of being connected upon arrival, allowing you to navigate to your accommodation and let your family know you have landed safely. Then, once you are settled, you can research and purchase a larger, more affordable local SIM card for the remainder of your stay, keeping the eSIM as a backup or for travel to neighboring countries.

Managing International Communication

Your connectivity plan extends beyond simple internet access. You also need a strategy for managing your personal and professional communication, primarily your phone number and messaging services, in a way that is both seamless and cost-effective.

The first challenge is what to do with your phone number from your home country. This number is often a critical key to your digital life, tied to your bank accounts, your email, and countless online services through two-factor authentication (2FA). Simply canceling your plan is not a viable option. One excellent solution, particularly for US-based nomads, is to port your existing number to a Voice over IP (VoIP) service like Google Voice. This process severs the link between your phone number and a physical SIM card, transforming it into a digital entity. You can then make and receive calls and texts to that number through a dedicated app on your smartphone, using either Wi-Fi or a mobile data connection. This allows you to maintain your critical home number from anywhere in the world for a very low cost.

If porting your number is not an option, you can often downgrade your home plan to the cheapest possible "pay as you go" or "talk and text" option. This keeps the number active for receiving essential 2FA text messages while you use a local or eSIM plan for your daily data needs.

For your day-to-day communication, you will quickly discover that traditional SMS text messaging and cellular calls are relics of a bygone era. The global language of communication is the data-based messaging app. WhatsApp is the undisputed global champion, a near-universal tool for communicating with friends, landlords, and businesses in most parts of the world. However, it is important to be aware of regional preferences. In countries like Japan and Thailand, LINE is the dominant platform. In Eastern Europe, Telegram has a strong foothold. And if you are planning to spend time in China, having WeChat is absolutely essential. A smart nomad has these key apps installed and set up before they arrive.

These apps are not just for texting. Their voice and video calling features, which run over data, allow you to have crystal-clear conversations with anyone in the world for free. When you do need to call a traditional landline or mobile number—for instance, to contact your bank's fraud department or to call a grandparent who doesn't use a smartphone—a VoIP service like Skype Out or Google Voice offers incredibly low per-minute rates, turning an expensive international call into a transaction that costs mere pennies.

Finally, many modern smartphones support a feature called Wi-Fi Calling. When enabled, this allows your phone to make and receive standard calls and texts over a Wi-Fi network instead of a cellular one. For a nomad, this is a powerful feature. It means that when you are connected to the Wi-Fi in your apartment in Bali, you can receive a call to your regular US phone number as if you were standing in your living room back home, often with no roaming charges.

By combining these strategies—a vetted primary Wi-Fi, a mobile hotspot backup powered by a flexible eSIM or local SIM, a ported home number, and a suite of data-based communication apps—you build a resilient and cost-effective connectivity system. You remove the uncertainty and anxiety around what is arguably the most critical piece of your nomadic infrastructure. This preparation allows your connection to fade into the background, becoming the reliable, invisible utility it should be, and freeing you to focus on the world waiting on the other side of your screen.

CHAPTER SIXTEEN: Building a Global Community and Overcoming Loneliness.

Of all the challenges a digital nomad faces—the scramble for reliable Wi-Fi, the labyrinth of visa applications, the tyranny of a variable income—none is more insidious or less discussed than the profound sense of loneliness that can creep in amidst a life of constant motion. We exist in a state of perpetual connection, our lives mediated through screens that link us to clients, colleagues, friends, and family across the globe. Yet, it is entirely possible to be surrounded by the vibrant chaos of a Bangkok market or the cheerful buzz of a Lisbon café and feel utterly, achingly alone. This is the great paradox of the nomadic life: you have the freedom to be anywhere, but you belong nowhere.

This chapter is about addressing that paradox head-on. The glossy social media feeds rarely show the quiet Saturday nights spent alone in a new apartment, the pang of seeing friends back home gather for a wedding, or the cumulative emotional fatigue of a thousand shallow conversations. Building a community on the move is not a passive activity that happens to you; it is an active, essential skill, as critical to your long-term sustainability as your ability to find work. Overcoming loneliness is about building a new kind of social framework, one that is as flexible, resilient, and intentional as the lifestyle itself.

The nature of nomadic relationships is inherently transient. You will meet incredible, fascinating people from all corners of the earth. You will form intense, accelerated friendships, sharing meals, adventures, and deep conversations over the course of a few weeks that might take years to develop back home. There is a unique and powerful bond that forms between people who have chosen a similar, unconventional path. These connections are real, they are meaningful, and they are one of the greatest gifts of this lifestyle. They are also, more often than not, temporary.

The nomadic life is a constant series of hellos and goodbyes. The friend you hiked a volcano with last weekend might be flying to a different continent next Tuesday. This revolving door of relationships can be emotionally taxing. It requires a mental shift, a letting go of the traditional model of a static, lifelong community of friends who live down the street. You must learn to appreciate the depth and beauty of a connection for what it is, without being crushed by the inevitability of its physical end. This is a skill that takes practice, patience, and a healthy dose of self-compassion.

The most effective way to combat the isolation of a new city is to proactively place yourself in environments designed for connection. Your first and most powerful tool in this endeavor is the co-working space. While its primary function is to provide a productive work environment, its secondary, and arguably equally important, function is to serve as a social hub. A co-working space is an instant collection of interesting, motivated people who are, just like you, looking to build a professional and social network in a new place. It is the modern-day village square for the location-independent.

To leverage a co-working space effectively, you must treat it as more than just a desk with good Wi-Fi. Arrive with a mindset of contribution and curiosity. Introduce yourself to the people sitting near you. Make a point of eating lunch in the communal kitchen rather than at your desk. Most importantly, attend the social events. Almost every co-working space organizes a calendar of activities, from weekly happy hours and skill-sharing workshops to group lunches and weekend excursions. These are not optional extras; they are the structured opportunities you need to turn a friendly nod into a genuine conversation.

An even more immersive option is the co-living arrangement. As we touched upon in Chapter Fourteen, co-living spaces are designed to be "community-in-a-box." By combining private living quarters with extensive shared amenities and organized events, they remove almost all the initial friction of building a social circle. Your housemates become your instant friends, your dinner companions, and your adventure partners. For a solo nomad, particularly one who is more introverted, the investment in a co-living space for the first month or two in a new city can be the single best antidote to loneliness.

The convenience of a ready-made community is undeniable. However, it is also important to be aware of the "nomad bubble." It is easy to spend all your time in co-working and co-living spaces, surrounded exclusively by other English-speaking foreigners. While these relationships are valuable, a truly rich nomadic experience involves stepping outside this bubble and engaging with the local culture and community. This requires a more deliberate and sometimes more challenging effort, but the rewards are a deeper sense of connection to the place you have chosen to call your temporary home.

One of the most effective ways to meet locals is by pursuing your existing hobbies or picking up a new one. Your passions are a universal language that can bridge cultural divides. Join a local CrossFit box, a yoga studio, a running club, or a pickup soccer league. Sign up for a pottery class, a dance lesson, or a cooking workshop. These activities create a context for repeated, low-pressure interaction with local residents who share your interests. The conversation starts with your shared activity, providing a natural and authentic foundation upon which a friendship can be built.

Language classes are another powerful tool for community building. Committing to learning even the basics of the local language shows a level of respect and engagement that will be deeply appreciated. Your classmates will be a mix of other foreigners and expatriates, providing another avenue for friendship. More importantly, your teacher and your stumbling attempts to practice your new skills in local shops and cafés will open doors to interactions that would otherwise be inaccessible. Even a simple "hello" and "thank you" in the local tongue can transform you from a passive observer into an active participant.

Volunteering is a profoundly rewarding way to connect with a community on a deeper level. Find a local organization whose mission resonates with you, whether it is an animal shelter, an environmental group, or a community center. Offering your time and skills without any expectation of financial reward is a powerful gesture of goodwill. It allows you to work alongside local people towards a common goal, fostering a unique sense of camaraderie and providing an intimate window into the culture and the real-world issues of the place you are living in.

The digital world, while sometimes a source of isolation, can also be your greatest ally in building an in-person community. The first step is to find the relevant online groups for your destination. Search on Facebook for terms like "[City Name] Expats," "[City Name] Digital Nomads," or "[Nationality] in [City Name]." These groups are a firehose of practical information, but they are also a hub for social organization. People use them to post about everything from informal coffee meetups and hiking trips to apartment shares and book clubs.

The platform Meetup.com is another invaluable resource, specifically designed to facilitate in-person gatherings around shared interests. You can find groups for almost anything imaginable, from board games and blockchain technology to urban sketching and vegetarian dinners. The key to using these online tools is to make the leap from digital to physical as quickly as possible. It is easy to become a passive "lurker" in these groups. The real value comes when you RSVP "yes" to an event and actually show up, even if you are nervous and do not know a single person there.

As you build your new, location-based community, it is equally important to nurture your relationships with the community you left behind. The nomadic life is a trade-off, and one of its sharpest edges is the inevitable "fear of missing out," or FOMO. While you are exploring a new corner of the world, life back home continues without you. Friends will get married, babies will be born, and inside jokes will be created that you are not a part of. Acknowledging and accepting this reality is the first step to managing it.

The key is to replace passive consumption of your friends' lives on social media with active, intentional connection. Scrolling through a feed of perfectly curated moments can amplify feelings of distance and loneliness. Instead, schedule regular, dedicated video calls. These one-on-one or small-group conversations are the digital equivalent of sitting down for a coffee. They allow for the nuance, depth, and genuine connection that a text message or a "like" on a photo can never replicate. Make these calls a non-negotiable part of your weekly routine.

Find creative ways to bridge the distance. Send postcards. Use an app to order a surprise coffee or a meal to be delivered to a friend on their birthday. Create a shared photo album or a group chat dedicated to more than just logistical updates. These small, consistent efforts demonstrate that even though you are physically distant, your relationships remain a priority. It is this active maintenance that keeps the roots of your home community strong, providing a vital sense of stability and belonging no matter where you are in the world.

Despite your best efforts, there will be days when loneliness hits. It is an unavoidable part of the emotional landscape of this lifestyle. The key is to recognize it, to name it, and to have a toolkit of strategies to address it without letting it spiral. The first and most important strategy is to learn to be your own best friend. The nomadic life involves a significant amount of solo time, and you must cultivate a genuine comfort with your own company. Learn to take yourself out on "dates"—a solo trip to a museum, a nice dinner with a book for company, a long walk through a park.

Create routines that provide a sense of structure and predictability to your day. This can be as simple as starting every morning with a walk to the same coffee shop or ending every workday with a short workout. These rituals act as anchors in a life of constant change, creating a comforting rhythm that can ward off feelings of aimlessness. When you feel a wave of loneliness coming on, having a plan of action is crucial. Do not sit and stew in the feeling. Change your environment. Go for a run, head to your co-working space even if you do not have work to do, or simply go to a busy public place like a library or a park.

Sometimes, the best antidote is to reach out proactively. When you are feeling lonely, it is a safe bet that another nomad somewhere in the same city is feeling the exact same way. Post a message in one of your online groups: "Hey, I'm new in town and fancy grabbing a coffee this afternoon. Anyone around?" The vulnerability of this simple act is often met with a warm and immediate response. You are not just solving your own problem; you are creating an opportunity for connection for someone else.

It is also vital to recognize the difference between a temporary bout of loneliness and more serious, persistent mental health challenges. The stresses of the nomadic lifestyle—the instability, the constant change, the distance from your established support systems—can exacerbate underlying issues like anxiety and depression. There is no shame in seeking professional help. The rise of online therapy platforms has made it easier than ever to connect with a qualified therapist for regular video sessions, providing a consistent source of support regardless of your location.

Over time, you will begin to build a new and beautiful kind of community, one that is not defined by a single geographical location. This is your global tribe. It is the collection of friends you have made in different cities, a network of couches to crash on and familiar faces to greet in airports around the world. It is the friend from your co-working space in Lisbon who you meet up with for a weekend in Berlin six months later. It is the family you house-sat for in Australia who you keep in touch with for years to come.

This global network becomes a profound source of joy and connection. You begin to see the world not just as a collection of places, but as a map of your relationships. While your local community may change with every new city, this global tribe remains a constant. Nurturing these long-distance friendships requires the same intentionality as maintaining your relationships back home. A quick message to check in, a shared article of interest, or a comment on a photo keeps the connection alive until your paths cross again.

Building a community on the road is a journey of its own, a parallel adventure to your physical travels. It requires courage— the courage to walk into a room full of strangers, to be the first one to say hello, to be vulnerable and to ask for connection. It requires patience, understanding that deep friendships take time to cultivate. And it requires intentionality, the conscious and continuous effort to seek out and nurture the human connections that transform a series of destinations into a rich and meaningful life.

CHAPTER SEVENTEEN: Health and Wellness on the Go: Staying Healthy While Traveling

The digital nomad lifestyle, as portrayed through the curated lens of social media, often looks like the pinnacle of well-being. It is a montage of yoga on the beach, acai bowls for breakfast, and tanned, smiling people who seem to have transcended the very concept of stress. While this vision contains elements of truth—the freedom from a soul-crushing commute is certainly a health benefit—the day-to-day reality of maintaining your physical and mental wellness on the road is a far more complex and deliberate undertaking. Your health is not a passive byproduct of this lifestyle; it is the foundational infrastructure upon which the entire enterprise is built.

A life in constant motion is inherently disruptive. It dismantles the routines that form the bedrock of a stable health regimen. There is no regular gym, no familiar running path, no well-stocked kitchen, and no consistent sleep schedule. You are constantly adapting to new climates, new foods, and new environmental stressors. This chapter is your practical guide to navigating these challenges. It is not about chasing an unattainable ideal of perfection, but about building a resilient, adaptable toolkit of habits and strategies that will allow you to feel strong, energized, and mentally balanced, no matter which time zone you wake up in. Think of your body not as a passenger on this journey, but as your most essential and irreplaceable piece of gear.

Physical Health on the Move

The most immediate challenge for many nomads is figuring out how to maintain a consistent fitness routine without a fixed address. The convenience of your neighborhood gym or your favorite spin class vanishes, replaced by a constantly shifting landscape of options. The key to success is to embrace flexibility and build a routine that is not dependent on a specific location or piece of equipment.

The most powerful tool in your fitness arsenal is your own body. Bodyweight fitness is the ultimate portable gym, a highly effective method for building strength and endurance that requires nothing more than a few square feet of floor space. A simple, well-rounded routine of squats, lunges, push-ups, and planks can be performed in any apartment, hotel room, or park in the world. Countless free resources on platforms like YouTube offer guided bodyweight workouts for all fitness levels, while apps can provide structured programs that keep you progressing. A commitment to a 20- or 30-minute bodyweight session three to four times a week can form the consistent core of your fitness plan.

For those looking to add a bit more resistance, a few carefully chosen pieces of portable gear can dramatically expand your workout options without weighing down your luggage. A set of resistance bands is incredibly lightweight and versatile, perfect for strength training and physical therapy exercises. A simple jump rope is an unparalleled tool for a high-intensity cardio workout. And for the more dedicated, a suspension trainer like a TRX can be anchored to a sturdy door or a tree branch, allowing for a full-body workout that rivals a session at a well-equipped gym.

Your new environment is not an obstacle to your fitness; it is your new playground. One of the greatest joys of arriving in a new city is exploring it on foot. Make walking your default mode of transportation. It is a low-impact form of exercise that allows you to discover hidden alleys, local markets, and the true rhythm of a place in a way that a subway or taxi ride never could. For a more intense workout, lacing up your running shoes and exploring a new city at dawn is a magical experience. Just be sure to research safe routes beforehand, and use an app that allows you to track your run without getting hopelessly lost.

When you crave the structure and community of a more traditional fitness environment, a little research will often reveal a wealth of options. The global fitness culture has made it easier than ever to be a temporary member of a local fitness tribe. Most yoga studios, CrossFit boxes, and martial arts dojos offer drop-in rates or one-week passes for visitors. This is not only a great way to get a workout but also an excellent opportunity to meet locals who share your interests. The cost of a few drop-in classes is a small investment in both your physical and social well-being.

Just as critical as your fitness is your nutrition. The temptation to treat a three-month stay in a new country like a three-month vacation can be overwhelming. Eating out for every meal is a fast track to draining your budget and feeling sluggish. The key to sustainable nutrition on the road is to find a healthy balance between indulging in the local cuisine and maintaining a baseline of home-cooked, nutritious meals.

A good guideline is the 80/20 rule: aim to prepare about 80% of your meals yourself, and reserve the other 20% for exploring the local restaurants, cafés, and street food stalls. This approach allows you to control the quality of your ingredients and your portion sizes for the majority of the time, while still fully engaging with the culinary culture of your new home. This requires a mental shift, reframing grocery shopping not as a chore, but as an adventure. Navigating a bustling local market, deciphering unfamiliar labels, and discovering new fruits and vegetables is a deeply immersive cultural experience.

Before you go shopping, take an inventory of your rental kitchen. Most short-term rentals will have the basics, but you will need to adapt your cooking style to what is available. Focus on simple, healthy meals that can be made in one or two pans. Omelets, stir-fries, lentil soups, and large salads are all nomad-friendly staples that are packed with nutrients and require minimal equipment. To make any temporary kitchen feel a bit more like home, consider creating a small, portable "pantry kit." This could be a small bag containing a few of your favorite essential spices, a good quality travel-sized olive oil, or your favorite brand of tea.

When you do eat out, you can still make mindful choices. Look for dishes that are grilled, steamed, or baked rather than fried. Load up on fresh vegetables and lean proteins. Street food, often the most authentic and delicious option, can also be surprisingly healthy if you choose wisely. Look for vendors with high turnover, as this is a good sign of freshness. And above all, listen to your body. The introduction of new ingredients and spices can sometimes be a shock to the system. Go slowly, pay attention to how you feel, and stay hydrated. A reusable water bottle with a built-in filter is an essential piece of gear, ensuring you always have access to safe, clean drinking water while reducing your plastic waste.

The final pillar of your physical health is sleep. The constant travel, changing time zones, and unfamiliar sleeping environments can wreak havoc on your sleep cycle. Prioritizing good sleep hygiene is not an indulgence; it is a prerequisite for productivity, a strong immune system, and a stable mood. Combating jet lag is the first battle. Try to gradually adjust your sleep schedule in the days leading up to a long flight. Once you arrive, resist the urge to take a long nap. Instead, expose yourself to natural sunlight as much as possible during the day, which helps to reset your internal clock.

You must become an expert at creating a portable sleep sanctuary. A high-quality sleep mask and a set of effective earplugs are non-negotiable items that can block out unwanted light and noise, the two biggest culprits of a poor night's sleep. A white noise app on your phone can be a lifesaver, masking the unfamiliar sounds of a new city. Even without a fixed bedroom, try to maintain a consistent wind-down routine. An hour before you plan to sleep, dim the lights, put away your screens, and do something relaxing like reading a book, listening to calm music, or doing some gentle stretching. This signals to your brain that it is time to prepare for rest.

Navigating Healthcare Systems Abroad

No matter how well you take care of yourself, there will come a time when you need medical attention. Navigating a foreign healthcare system can be an intimidating prospect, especially when you are feeling unwell and may be facing a language barrier. The key to managing this is preparation. Your healthcare strategy should be in place long before you ever feel the first symptom.

Your preparation should begin at home with a pre-travel check-up. Visit your primary care physician and your dentist for a clean bill of health before you embark on a long period of travel. This is the time to refill any prescription medications and to get any necessary vaccinations. Check the Centers for Disease Control and Prevention (CDC) or the World Health Organization (WHO) websites for the specific health recommendations and vaccination requirements for your planned destinations.

If you rely on prescription medication, you must plan meticulously. Aim to travel with enough medication to last your entire trip, plus a little extra in case of delays. Always keep your medication in its original packaging with the pharmacy label clearly visible. It is also crucial to carry a signed letter from your doctor that explains your condition and the medication you need. Before you travel, research the legality of your specific medication in your destination country. Some substances that are common prescriptions in one country can be considered controlled substances in another.

You should also assemble a comprehensive personal first-aid kit. This should go beyond a few bandages and an antiseptic wipe. Include a good supply of any over-the-counter medications you use regularly, such as painkillers, antihistamines, or allergy relief. Add items like rehydration salts for treating dehydration, hydrocortisone cream for insect bites, and a broad-spectrum antibiotic prescribed by your doctor for emergencies. Having these items on hand can turn a minor ailment into a non-issue, saving you the stress of trying to find a pharmacy in the middle of the night.

The most critical component of your healthcare plan is your insurance. As we have stressed before, traveling without comprehensive travel medical insurance is an act of extreme financial recklessness. A serious illness or accident abroad can lead to medical bills that are genuinely bankrupting. Be clear on the distinction between the basic travel insurance that might come with your credit card (which typically covers trip cancellation and lost luggage) and a dedicated travel medical insurance policy, which is what you need.

When choosing a policy, read the fine print carefully. Look for a plan with a high coverage limit for medical expenses and, most importantly, a provision for emergency medical evacuation. This covers the astronomical cost of transporting you to a better-equipped hospital or back to your home country if necessary. Ensure the policy covers the countries you plan to visit and any "adventure sports" like skiing or scuba diving that you might engage in. Keep a digital and a physical copy of your insurance policy information with you at all times.

When you do need to find medical care on the ground, you have several resources at your disposal. Your insurance provider will often have a 24/7 assistance line that can refer you to reputable, pre-approved doctors and hospitals in their network. The U.S. embassy or the consulate of your home country in your destination often maintains a list of recommended English-speaking doctors and dentists. Online communities, like local expat Facebook groups, can also be an invaluable source for personal recommendations. In a non-emergency situation, the rise of telemedicine services offers a convenient first step, allowing you to have a video consultation with a qualified doctor without leaving your apartment.

Navigating a pharmacy in a foreign country can be its own adventure. The names of drugs can vary, and what is available over-the-counter in your home country might require a prescription, and vice-versa. Having a translation app on your phone is essential for communicating your symptoms. It is also helpful to know the generic, scientific name of any medication you need, as this is more universal than the brand name.

Mental and Emotional Wellness

The constant flux of the nomadic lifestyle, while exhilarating, can also take a significant toll on your mental and emotional well-being. The lack of a stable home base, the constant decision-making, and the distance from your established support network can create a unique form of stress. Maintaining your mental health requires the same level of conscious effort and intentionality as maintaining your physical health.

As we have discussed, routine is a powerful anchor in a life of change. While your macro-routine is constantly shifting, you can create a set of "micro-routines" that provide a comforting sense of predictability. This could be a five-minute meditation session every morning, a daily walk to the same coffee shop, or the ritual of making a cup of tea every afternoon before you wrap up your workday. These small, consistent actions create a scaffold of stability that can help you feel more grounded.

Mindfulness and meditation are not just buzzwords; they are practical, portable tools for managing the mental chatter and stress that can accompany this lifestyle. A few minutes of focused breathing can be a powerful reset button during a stressful day. Apps like Headspace or Calm offer guided meditations that can be done anywhere, from an airport gate to your apartment bedroom.

Journaling is another incredibly effective practice for a nomad. Your life will be a firehose of new experiences, sights, and emotions. The act of writing them down helps you to process this constant influx of information. It provides a private space to work through challenges, celebrate small victories, and prevent the days and weeks from blurring into an indistinguishable mass. Your journal becomes a tangible record of your personal growth and a cherished souvenir of your journey.

It is also vital to recognize the signs of burnout. This is more than just feeling tired; it is a state of emotional, physical, and mental exhaustion. The symptoms can include a deep sense of cynicism about your work and travels, a feeling of being constantly drained, and a lack of motivation. When you feel burnout approaching, the solution is not to push harder. It is to give yourself permission to rest. This might mean taking a "vacation from your travel." Book a comfortable apartment for a week or two, unpack completely, and do nothing. Cook familiar food, watch your favorite shows, and sleep. This is not a sign of failure; it is a necessary act of strategic recovery.

Finally, do not hesitate to seek professional support. The stigma around mental health is fading, and the rise of online therapy has made it more accessible than ever. A regular video call with a therapist can provide a consistent, confidential, and professional source of support, a stable anchor you can rely on no matter where you are in the world. Your mental and emotional wellness is not a secondary concern. It is the very lens through which you experience your life, your work, and your travels. Investing in it is the most important investment you will ever make.

CHAPTER EIGHTEEN: Cultural Etiquette and Making a Positive Impact

Your arrival in a new country is a transaction. You exchange your money for food, lodging, and experiences. For many travelers, this is where the relationship with their destination begins and ends. They remain a customer, an observer looking through a window at the life of a place. But the digital nomad is not a typical traveler. You are not on a two-week vacation; you are a temporary resident, a guest in someone else's home for a month, or three, or six. This extended stay comes with a deeper responsibility and a far greater opportunity: the chance to move beyond the transactional and build a relationship of mutual respect with the culture that is hosting you.

This chapter is about the practical art of being a good guest. It is about understanding that cultural norms are not obstacles to be overcome, but a different and valid way of viewing the world. Mastering the basics of cultural etiquette is not about memorizing a rigid list of rules to avoid embarrassment. It is a proactive expression of respect that opens doors to more authentic connections and a richer experience. Furthermore, it is about recognizing that your presence has an impact. Your choices— where you spend your money, how you consume resources, and how you interact with the community—collectively shape the perception of the digital nomad movement and determine whether it is a force for good or a source of friction.

The Foundation: Shut Up and Watch

The single most valuable skill for navigating a new culture is the ability to be quiet and observant. In the first few days in a new city, resist the urge to impose your own habits and assumptions. Instead, become an anthropologist of daily life. Find a bench in a busy square or a seat in a local, non-touristy café, and simply watch. How do people greet each other? A handshake? A nod? A kiss on the cheek? How do they queue for a bus—in a neat line or a fluid crowd? What is the ambient volume of a conversation in a restaurant? How much personal space do they leave between each other when they talk?

This period of quiet observation is your primary data-gathering phase. You will learn more about the unspoken rules of a society by watching how locals interact with each other than you ever could from a guidebook. Pay attention to body language. A gesture that is innocuous in your home country could be offensive in another. Eye contact is another crucial cue; in some cultures, direct eye contact is a sign of honesty and confidence, while in others it can be perceived as aggressive or disrespectful, particularly when directed at an elder. Your initial goal is not to participate, but to calibrate your own behavior to the local baseline.

This principle extends to your speech. Many native English speakers, particularly Americans, are accustomed to a certain level of volume and directness in their communication. In many other cultures, especially in Asia and parts of Europe, a loud voice in a public space is considered abrasive and inconsiderate. Be mindful of your own volume on public transport, in restaurants, and even in your co-working space. The simple act of lowering your voice by a few decibels can be a significant gesture of cultural awareness and respect.

You must also observe the local concept of time. The Western, particularly North American and Northern European, view of time is often "monochronic." Time is a finite resource that is managed, scheduled, and segmented. Punctuality is a virtue, and being late for a business meeting or even a social engagement is a sign of disrespect. However, a huge portion of the world operates on a "polychronic" concept of time. In many Latin American, African, and Middle Eastern cultures, relationships and social interactions are often prioritized over rigid schedules. Time is more fluid. An invitation for dinner at 8 PM might mean it is perfectly acceptable, even expected, for you to arrive at 8:30 PM or later. Applying a monochronic expectation of punctuality in a polychronic culture can lead to unnecessary frustration for you and can make you appear impatient and rigid to your hosts.

The Daily Practice: Navigating Social Norms

With a foundation of observation, you can begin to engage with the local culture more confidently. This requires a conscious effort to adapt your daily habits to the norms of your new environment. The most basic and powerful tool in this endeavor is language. You do not need to become fluent, but learning a few key phrases is non-negotiable. Mastering "hello," "goodbye," "please," "thank you," and "excuse me" in the local language is the minimum standard of politeness. It is a small effort that signals a huge amount of respect. Write these phrases down phonetically in a note on your phone and practice them. The smile you receive in return for a fumbling but sincere attempt to speak the local language is one of the great rewards of this lifestyle.

Dining etiquette is a vast and varied landscape where it is easy to make a misstep. In some parts of the world, it is considered rude to rest your elbows on the table; in others, it is rude to have your hands in your lap. Research the local customs around utensils. Is it acceptable to eat with your hands? If so, is there a rule about using only your right hand? The concept of tipping is another minefield. In the United States, a generous tip is expected and forms a major part of a server's income. In many European countries, a service charge is already included, and a small additional tip is a gesture of appreciation for excellent service, not an obligation. In Japan, tipping is not a part of the culture and can be considered confusing or even insulting.

The question of how to dress is about more than just personal style; it is a form of non-verbal communication. What you wear sends a message about your respect for the local culture. A good rule of thumb is to observe how the locals dress in a similar context and aim for that level of modesty, or one step more conservative. Clothing that is perfectly acceptable on a beach in Bali might be deeply inappropriate for walking through the city streets of Marrakech. When visiting any place of worship—a temple, a mosque, or a cathedral—the rules of modesty are paramount. This almost always means covering your shoulders and knees, and sometimes your head. Carrying a lightweight scarf or sarong in your daypack is a simple and effective way to ensure you are always prepared to dress appropriately.

If you are fortunate enough to be invited into someone's home, it is a significant gesture of hospitality that comes with its own set of expectations. It is almost always appropriate to bring a small gift for your hosts. However, the choice of gift can be nuanced. A bottle of wine is a common gift in many Western cultures, but it would be inappropriate to bring to the home of a Muslim family. Do some quick research. Are flowers a good gift, and if so, are there certain colors or numbers of flowers that have negative connotations? When you arrive, you may be asked to remove your shoes. Look for a pile of shoes by the door—this is your cue. Always accept any offer of food or drink, as refusing can sometimes be seen as a rejection of your host's hospitality.

You must also learn to navigate the subtleties of communication. In many "high-context" cultures, particularly in Asia and the Middle East, communication is indirect. Meaning is conveyed through context, body language, and what is *not* said, rather than through direct words. A direct "no" can be considered confrontational and rude. Instead of refusing a request, someone might say "I will see what I can do" or "That may be difficult." Learning to read these subtle cues is a skill that takes time to develop. In these contexts, it is wise to soften your own communication. Instead of making direct demands, phrase your requests more gently and be prepared for ambiguous answers.

Finally, be a mindful photographer. The people and places you encounter are not props for your social media feed. It is a fundamental violation of respect to shove a camera in a stranger's face without their permission. If you want to take a portrait, make eye contact, smile, and gesture to your camera. A nod of assent is your permission; a shake of the head or a turned back must be respected without question. Be particularly sensitive when photographing children or in situations that involve poverty or hardship. Ask yourself if your photograph is honoring the dignity of the subject or exploiting their circumstances for "likes."

The Nomad's Footprint: Leaving a Place Better Than You Found It

Being a good guest goes beyond polite interactions. It involves a conscious awareness of the economic, social, and environmental impact of your presence. As a digital nomad, you are part of a privileged global minority. Your ability to earn a strong currency while living in a more affordable country gives you significant economic power. Wielding that power responsibly is a core tenet of being a positive force in the world.

The most direct way to make a positive economic impact is to ensure your money supports the local community directly. Make a conscious choice to frequent locally-owned businesses rather than international chains. Buy your groceries from the neighborhood market instead of the large supermarket. Eat at family-run restaurants, get your coffee from the independent café on the corner, and hire local guides for your weekend excursions. This ensures that the money you spend circulates within the community you are living in, rather than being siphoned off to a corporate headquarters in another country.

This principle extends to how you pay for goods and services. In many cultures, haggling is a normal and expected part of a transaction, particularly in open-air markets. It can be a fun and engaging social ritual. However, it is important to understand the context. There is a vast difference between friendly bargaining over a souvenir and aggressively haggling with a vegetable vendor over a few cents. Remember that the small amount of money that is trivial to you could be significant to the person you are buying from. The goal is to arrive at a fair price, not to "win" the negotiation at all costs.

Your social footprint is just as important as your economic one. The influx of a large number of foreigners into a desirable neighborhood can have unintended consequences, a phenomenon often referred to as "nomad gentrification." The increased demand for short-term rentals can drive up housing prices, making it more difficult for local residents to afford to live in their own communities. While you are not solely responsible for these market forces, you can make more mindful choices. Consider staying in neighborhoods that are slightly outside the main tourist and expat bubble. Engage with the local community in ways that are not purely transactional.

Learning the language, even at a basic conversational level, is the single most powerful way to bridge the social divide. It demonstrates a genuine investment in the culture and opens up the possibility of forming real friendships with local people. It allows you to move beyond the "expat bubble" and gain a much deeper understanding of the place you are in. When you do discuss local issues, do so with humility and a desire to learn. Avoid making sweeping judgments or comparing everything to your home country. Your role is not to be a critic, but to be an informed and respectful observer.

Finally, you must be mindful of your environmental footprint. A life of constant air travel is inherently carbon-intensive. While you cannot eliminate this impact entirely, you can make more sustainable choices in your daily life. The easiest and most impactful habit is to eliminate single-use plastics. Carry a reusable water bottle (with a filter if necessary), a reusable coffee cup, and a set of foldable shopping bags. In many countries, the infrastructure for waste management and recycling is not as robust as what you may be used to. Be conscious of your consumption and try to produce as little waste as possible.

Be a mindful consumer of utilities in your rental apartment. Water and electricity are precious resources in many parts of the world. Do not take excessively long showers or leave the air conditioning blasting when you are not in the room. When you venture out into natural spaces like beaches, parks, and hiking trails, adhere strictly to the principles of "Leave No Trace." Pack out everything you pack in, stay on designated trails to avoid eroding the landscape, and do not disturb the local wildlife.

Being a culturally aware and responsible nomad is not about achieving a perfect, flawless performance. You will make mistakes. You will accidentally use the wrong greeting, misunderstand a social cue, or commit a minor faux pas. When this happens, the best response is a humble smile and a sincere apology. Most people are incredibly forgiving and will appreciate your effort, even if it is clumsy. The goal is not perfection, but intention. It is the conscious and continuous effort to move through the world with respect, curiosity, and a genuine desire to leave a positive wake behind you. This is what transforms a simple trip into a meaningful exchange, enriching not only your own life but also the communities that so generously welcome you.

CHAPTER NINETEEN: Productivity and Time Management Across Time Zones

The freedom to design your own workday is one of the most powerful and seductive promises of the digital nomad lifestyle. The rigid, externally imposed structure of the nine-to-five is gone, replaced by a blank canvas of twenty-four hours that you, and you alone, get to fill. This is the ultimate expression of professional autonomy. It is also, for the unprepared, a surefire recipe for chaos, anxiety, and a spectacular nosedive in productivity. When your office is a different café every week and your colleagues are scattered across a dozen time zones, the traditional anchors of a workday—the commute, the shared lunch break, the boss walking past your desk—all vanish. You are left floating in a sea of unstructured time, with the siren song of a new city to explore constantly calling from the shore.

This chapter is your guide to building a new set of anchors. It is not about finding a magic formula or a single productivity "hack" that will solve all your problems. It is about becoming the architect of your own professional life, consciously designing a system of habits, routines, and boundaries that works for your unique brain and your specific professional obligations. The goal is to move beyond a state of constant, low-grade reactivity—answering emails as they arrive, hopping on calls whenever they are requested—and into a state of intentional, proactive control. True freedom is not the absence of structure; it is the ability to create your own.

The first step is to dismantle the romantic but destructive myth of the four-hour workweek. While a few individuals have built businesses that allow for such a schedule, for the vast majority of digital nomads—the freelancers, the remote employees, the early-stage entrepreneurs—this is a dangerous fantasy. Most successful nomads work full-time hours, and often more. The difference is not in the quantity of work, but in the quality and the timing. The nomad's superpower is not working less; it is the ability to perform high-value, focused work in concentrated bursts, freeing up the rest of their time for exploration and life. This is the principle of "deep work."

Coined by the author Cal Newport, deep work is the ability to focus without distraction on a cognitively demanding task. It is the state of flow where you are fully immersed, pushing your cognitive capabilities to their limit and producing work of the highest quality and value. This is the work that gets you promoted, wins you high-paying clients, and builds your business. The opposite is "shallow work": the non-cognitively demanding, logistical tasks that are often performed while distracted. This is the world of answering emails, responding to Slack messages, and attending status update meetings. While necessary, shallow work creates very little new value in the world.

In a traditional office, the environment is often a constant engine of shallow work, with interruptions and distractions being the norm. As a nomad, you have a unique opportunity to design your life around deep work. Your primary productivity challenge is to ruthlessly protect your time and attention for these deep work sessions and to batch the shallow work into specific, contained windows. The freelancer who can write a brilliant marketing strategy in a three-hour, uninterrupted block is infinitely more valuable—and has far more free time—than the one who takes eight hours to do the same task while being constantly distracted by notifications and the lure of social media.

This deep work philosophy is the foundation upon which you will build your daily schedule. This does not mean creating a rigid, minute-by-minute itinerary that you must follow like a soldier. Your life is too fluid for that. Instead, it is about creating a flexible template, a default rhythm for your day that you can adapt to your location and your energy levels. The first step in creating this template is to understand your own biological clock, your chronotype. Your energy and focus are not constant throughout the day; they ebb and flow in a predictable pattern. Designing your workday in opposition to this natural rhythm is like trying to swim against a strong current—you can do it, but it is exhausting and inefficient.

Researchers have identified several chronotypes, but they can be broadly simplified. Are you a "lion," an early bird who is most alert and productive in the morning, from around 8 AM to noon? Or are you a "wolf," a night owl who does their best creative thinking late in the evening? Perhaps you are a "bear," whose energy cycle follows the sun, with a predictable dip in the mid-afternoon. Understanding your chronotype is a game-changer. It allows you to schedule your most important, cognitively demanding deep work during your natural peak performance window. A lion should protect their mornings at all costs for deep work, while a wolf should not force themselves to tackle a complex problem at 9 AM.

Once you know when you are at your best, you can begin to structure your day using a technique called time blocking. This is the practice of dividing your day into specific blocks of time and assigning a single task or type of task to each block. Instead of working from a chaotic to-do list, you are giving every minute of your workday a job. Your calendar becomes your map for the day. A lion's time-blocked schedule might look something like this: 8 AM to 11 AM is a "Deep Work" block dedicated to a single, high-priority project. 11 AM to 12 PM is a "Shallow Work" block for clearing emails. After lunch and a mid-afternoon energy dip, 2 PM to 4 PM might be a block for client calls, which are less cognitively demanding.

A more advanced version of this strategy is to organize your entire week with themed days. This is particularly effective for freelancers and entrepreneurs who wear many different hats. For example, Monday could be your "CEO Day," dedicated to business planning, strategy, and financial admin. Tuesday and Wednesday could be your "Deep Work Days," with your schedule cleared for focused, client-facing work. Thursday could be your "Marketing Day," focused on writing blog posts, updating your portfolio, and networking. Friday could be your "Meeting Day," where you batch all your client calls and check-ins. This approach prevents context-switching, the mental drag that comes from constantly shifting between different types of tasks, allowing you to build momentum and focus on one area of your business at a time.

Of course, your personal productivity system does not exist in a vacuum. It must interface with the schedules of your clients and colleagues, which brings us to the central challenge: the time zone tango. For the remote employee, this dance is often the most complex. Your ability to work effectively depends on finding a balance between your own ideal schedule and the company's need for collaboration. The key is to establish clear and explicit "core hours." These are a small, pre-agreed-upon window of time— perhaps two to three hours a day—where your schedule overlaps with that of your team. This is the dedicated time for synchronous communication: the daily stand-up meeting, the quick brainstorming session, the urgent questions that need a real-time answer.

Outside of these core hours, the expectation should be that communication is asynchronous. This requires a shift in mindset for the entire team. It means trusting that your colleagues are working, even when their Slack status is inactive. It means getting comfortable with a response time that might be several hours, not several minutes. Your responsibility during your working hours is to be as productive as possible and to end your day with a clear and concise "hand-off." This could be a detailed update on a project management tool or a summary email that allows your colleague in London to wake up and immediately understand the status of a project you were working on in Bali.

For freelancers, managing the time zone tango is about proactively setting client expectations from the very beginning of a relationship. Your location is not an apology; it is a simple logistical fact. Be upfront in your initial conversations. Your email signature and website should clearly state your current time zone. When a client asks when you can get something done, be specific: "I can have that for you by the end of my workday on Tuesday, which is 9 AM Wednesday your time." This clarity prevents misunderstandings and demonstrates your professionalism.

One of the most powerful tools for managing this is an online scheduling app like Calendly or SavvyCal. These tools sync with your calendar and allow you to set your availability. When a client wants to book a meeting, you simply send them a link. The tool automatically detects their time zone and shows them only the available slots that work for both of you. This eliminates the endless, frustrating chain of emails trying to find a mutually convenient time. It is a small piece of automation that saves hours of administrative headache and makes you appear incredibly organized.

To execute this well-designed schedule, you need a toolkit of techniques for managing your focus in a world of infinite distractions. One of the most simple and effective is the Pomodoro Technique. The method is straightforward: you set a timer for 25 minutes and work on a single task with absolute, single-minded focus. When the timer goes off, you take a five-minute break to stretch, get some water, or look out the window. After four of these "pomodoros," you take a longer break of 15 to 30 minutes. This technique is brilliant because it breaks down a daunting, three-hour deep work block into manageable, bite-sized intervals. The 25-minute deadline creates a gentle sense of urgency, and the built-in breaks prevent burnout and help to reset your focus.

Just as important as how you start your work is how you end it. The lack of a physical commute means there is no natural separation between your work life and your personal life. It is dangerously easy for the two to bleed into each other, with work expanding to fill all available time. To combat this, you must create your own boundaries in the form of rituals. A "work trigger" is a small ritual that signals to your brain that it is time to start the workday. This could be as simple as making a specific type of coffee, changing out of your pajamas, or walking once around the block before you sit down at your laptop.

Even more crucial is the "shutdown ritual." This is a consistent routine you perform at the end of your workday to signal that you are officially "off the clock." It should involve a series of simple, repeatable steps. You might, for example, review your to-do list for the day, create a plan for the next day, close all work-related tabs on your computer, say a specific phrase like "shutdown complete," and then physically close your laptop and put it away in your bag. This act of putting your office "to bed" creates a powerful psychological boundary. The workday is over. You are now free, without guilt, to go and enjoy your evening.

These rituals are a defense against the greatest enemy of productivity: notifications. The constant pings, dings, and red bubbles from email, Slack, and social media are a relentless assault on your focus. Each tiny interruption, even if you do not act on it, breaks your concentration and requires significant mental energy to recover from. You must be ruthless in taming this beast. During your deep work blocks, turn off all notifications on your phone and your computer. Close your email and Slack tabs. The world can wait for three hours. The fear that you will miss something urgent is almost always an illusion. In a true emergency, someone will call you. By batching your email and Slack checks into your designated "shallow work" blocks, you reclaim control over your attention.

The ultimate challenge for the productive nomad is managing the seductive blur between work and life. The very thing that makes this lifestyle so appealing—the ability to work from a beautiful location—is also what can make it so unproductive. If you are constantly feeling like you should be exploring while you are working, and feeling guilty about work while you are exploring, you will fail at both. This is the "work-life bleed," and it is a major cause of burnout.

The solution is to be as intentional about scheduling your leisure as you are about scheduling your work. Put your adventures on your calendar. A time block for "Hike to the waterfall" or "Explore the Old Town" is just as legitimate and important as a block for "Write client proposal." This gives you permission to fully disconnect and be present in your experience, knowing that your work time is also protected.

You must also learn to resist the "workcation" trap. It is tempting to believe you can effectively work while also being on a trip with friends or family who are in full vacation mode. In reality, this often leads to you doing a poor job of working and a poor job of vacationing. It is far better to be clear about your boundaries. Take a few full days off to be completely present with your visitors, and then schedule a few full days where you are completely focused on work, perhaps in a co-working space away from the vacation vibes.

Finally, consider using your physical location as a productivity tool. You can create location-based boundaries that help to prime your brain for a specific type of task. Your apartment, for example, could be a place of rest and light administrative work. A specific quiet café could be your designated spot for creative writing. The focused, professional environment of a co-working space could be reserved for your most critical deep work sessions. By associating a specific physical space with a specific type of mental work, you create powerful psychological cues that make it easier to slip into a state of focus.

Ultimately, productivity as a digital nomad is a continuous experiment. What works for you in a bustling city might need to be adapted for a quiet beach town. The key is to be a curious and compassionate scientist of your own habits. Pay attention to your energy, track your time, and be honest about what is working and what is not. By building a robust, adaptable system, you transform time from a relentless master into a flexible and powerful ally, allowing you to deliver exceptional work while fully embracing the extraordinary freedom you have earned.

CHAPTER TWENTY: The Art of Asynchronous Communication

In the grand theater of a traditional office, the workday is a relentless, unscripted performance of synchronous action. It is a world of shoulder-taps, of "got a quick second?" interruptions, of meetings called to prepare for other meetings. Communication is expected to be instantaneous, and a quick response is often valued more highly than a thoughtful one. This culture of immediacy is the invisible cage of the nine-to-five, the force that chains you not just to a desk, but to a specific nine-hour block of time. As a digital nomad, you have been handed the key to this cage. The key is asynchronous communication.

This is not simply a fancy term for a time-delayed conversation. It is a fundamental paradigm shift in how we approach collaboration. Asynchronous communication, or "async," is not a compromise born from the inconvenience of time zones; it is a deliberate and, for many types of work, a superior way of operating. It is the art of moving projects forward without the need for everyone to be present and available at the exact same moment. Mastering this art is the final, critical step in decoupling your work from your location, transforming time from a rigid constraint into a flexible and powerful asset. It is the skill that allows a developer in Bali to collaborate seamlessly with a designer in Berlin and a client in San Francisco, all while preserving the long, uninterrupted stretches of focus required for high-quality work.

The first principle of async is a radical recalibration of the word "urgent." In a synchronous environment, every ping and notification is treated as an emergency, a demand for your immediate attention. This creates a state of constant, low-grade anxiety and makes deep, concentrated work all but impossible. The async-first mindset begins with the assumption that very few things are truly urgent. A problem that requires an immediate, all-hands-on-deck response is a rare exception, not the daily norm. This allows you to reclaim your time, to work on your own schedule, and to engage with communications on your own terms. It requires a collective agreement to respect each other's focus and to trust that a response will come, just not necessarily in the next five minutes.

For this system to function, trust must be the default setting. The async world has no room for micromanagers. There is no way to digitally replicate the act of walking around an office to see who is "at their desk." The green dot next to a name in a chat app is a meaningless and often misleading metric of productivity. In an asynchronous culture, you are trusted to be a professional. You are trusted to manage your own time, to do your work to a high standard, and to be accountable for your output. Your value is measured by the quality and timeliness of what you produce, not by your perceived availability or the speed of your response to a message. This shift from presence to output is the cultural foundation upon which all successful remote teams are built.

With this trust comes a new level of personal responsibility. In an office, it is easy to become reliant on the immediate availability of others. When you hit a roadblock, you can simply ask the person next to you. In an async environment, your first question should never be directed at a colleague, but at yourself: "Have I done everything I can to solve this on my own?" This fosters a culture of initiative and resourcefulness. Before you ask a question, you are expected to have checked the company's internal documentation, performed a thorough search, and brainstormed a few potential solutions. You transition from being a simple asker of questions to a proactive presenter of solutions.

The engine of this self-reliance is documentation. When you cannot tap someone on the shoulder, you need a single, reliable place to find answers. In an async company, documentation is not a tedious administrative task; it is a core part of the product. Every project should have a clear brief, every process should be written down, and every important decision should be recorded in a shared, accessible space. This "single source of truth"—be it a company wiki, a well-organized project management tool, or a shared folder of documents—becomes the collective brain of the team. It is an investment that pays huge dividends, reducing repetitive questions, speeding up the onboarding of new members, and allowing anyone to get up to speed on a project at any time.

This new way of working requires a new way of communicating, a level of clarity and detail that can feel like overkill at first. This is the principle of over-communication. In a face-to-face conversation, you can rely on tone, body language, and immediate follow-up questions to fill in the gaps. In an async message, there are no gaps. You must anticipate the questions your colleagues might have and answer them in your initial message. The lazy synchronous message of "Hey, you there?" is a cardinal sin in the async world. It forces the other person to respond simply to find out what you want, creating a needless interruption.

A good async message is a self-contained package of information. It starts with a clear subject line or an introductory sentence that states the purpose. It provides all necessary context, including links to relevant documents, a summary of the issue, and the specific action you need from the other person. For example, instead of "Can you look at the new design?", a good async message would be: "Feedback needed on V2 of the homepage mockup for Project Phoenix by EOD Tuesday. Here is the Figma link. I'm specifically looking for feedback on the new CTA button placement and the hero image selection. The project brief with our goals is linked here for context." This single, detailed message allows the designer to provide thoughtful feedback on their own schedule, without a single follow-up question.

The tools you use every day must be adapted to this new philosophy. Email, the original asynchronous tool, regains its power when used correctly. A well-written email has a specific and searchable subject line. It is concise, with a clear "ask" or call to action. Long, sprawling email chains are a sign of a broken process. When a decision is reached, one person should be responsible for summarizing the outcome to end the thread. This creates a clean, documented record for anyone who needs to reference it later.

Messaging apps like Slack or Microsoft Teams are the most common source of asynchronous friction. They are often used as real-time chat rooms, destroying focus with a constant stream of notifications. To use them effectively, you must be disciplined. First, ruthlessly manage your notifications. Turn off all non-essential alerts. Second, use threads. A new question should never be a new message in a main channel; it should be a reply in a relevant thread. This keeps conversations organized and prevents the main channel from becoming an unreadable wall of text. Third, use status updates to signal your availability. A status of "Deep Work until 3 PM" or "On a client call" is a simple, effective way to manage your colleagues' expectations.

Your project management software—be it Asana, Trello, Jira, or a similar tool—is the true backbone of your asynchronous workflow. It is your shared workspace, your communication log, and your source of truth. A task in a project management tool should be treated with the same care as a detailed email. A task titled "Update website" is useless. A well-written task is titled "Update the 'About Us' page with the new team bios." It is assigned to a specific person, it has a clear deadline, and the description contains all the necessary information, including the text for the new bios and a link to the staging site. When you finish your part of the work, you update the task, attach the relevant files, and reassign it to the next person in the chain. This is the digital equivalent of passing a baton in a relay race, a clean and clear hand-off that allows the project to move forward seamlessly across time zones.

One of the most powerful and underutilized tools in the async toolkit is the pre-recorded video message. A five-minute video, created with a tool like Loom, can often replace a thirty-minute meeting. Instead of trying to find a time for a live screen-share, you can record yourself walking through a design mockup, explaining a piece of code, or giving feedback on a document. You can talk and point to your screen, providing all the nuance and visual context of a live call, but on your own schedule. The recipient can then watch the video at their convenience, absorb the information at their own pace, and leave time-stamped comments with their questions. This is an incredibly efficient and respectful way to communicate complex ideas.

Shared, collaborative documents are the final piece of the puzzle. Platforms like Google Docs and Notion are the virtual whiteboards where ideas are developed and refined. The key to using them effectively is to establish a clear workflow for feedback. Instead of sending around different versions of a Word document and trying to reconcile the changes, everyone works on a single, living document. Changes are made using the "suggesting" mode, and questions or comments are left directly on the relevant text. This creates a transparent record of the feedback process and ensures that everyone is always working from the most current version.

This asynchronous-first approach will inevitably lead you to question the necessity of most meetings. The default impulse in a synchronous culture is to call a meeting to solve a problem. In an async culture, the first question is always: "Can we resolve this without a meeting?" Most status updates can be a written post. Most feedback sessions can be a series of comments on a document. Most informational presentations can be a pre-recorded video. By aggressively filtering out unnecessary meetings, you reclaim hundreds of hours of precious time for focused, productive work.

Of course, some meetings are necessary. Synchronous, real-time conversation is still the best medium for complex brainstorming, sensitive personnel discussions, and building personal rapport. However, an async-friendly meeting is structured very differently from a traditional one. It begins with a clear and detailed agenda, sent out at least 24 hours in advance. This agenda is not just a list of topics; it is a set of questions to be answered. It includes links to all necessary pre-reading materials, with the explicit expectation that all attendees will have reviewed them beforehand. The meeting itself is reserved for discussion and decision-making, not for the initial presentation of information.

During the meeting, one person should be designated as the note-taker, capturing the key points of the discussion and, most importantly, the final decisions and action items. These notes should be cleaned up and shared with all attendees (and any relevant stakeholders who could not attend) within an hour of the meeting's conclusion. For critical meetings, it is also a good practice to record them, allowing team members in drastically different time zones to watch the discussion later. This level of discipline transforms a meeting from a time-wasting information dump into a focused and effective decision-making session.

As a freelancer, you have the power to gently guide your clients toward a more asynchronous way of working. This starts with the onboarding process. Clearly state your working hours and your preferred methods of communication. Instead of offering unlimited phone calls, establish a process: "For non-urgent questions, email is best. For project feedback, please leave comments directly on the shared document. If we do need to chat, you can book a time on my calendar here." By providing clear, easy-to-use systems, you make it simple for them to respect your time and focus. Your consistent, reliable, and high-quality work, delivered on time without the need for constant check-ins, will be the most powerful proof that this system works.

If you are a remote employee, you can be a powerful agent of change within your team. Lead by example. Write the kind of detailed, thoughtful messages that you want to receive. Be the person who always creates a clear agenda before a meeting. When someone asks to "hop on a quick call," gently challenge the request: "Happy to, but to make sure we're prepared, could you share a few bullet points on what you'd like to discuss? It might be something we can sort out right here in the thread." This is not about being difficult; it is about championing a more efficient and respectful way of working for everyone.

Adopting an asynchronous mindset is not without its challenges. It can feel isolating at first. You may miss the easy camaraderie and spontaneous brainstorming of an office. This is a real trade-off, and it is why building intentional social connections, as we have discussed, is so important. You may also feel a sense of anxiety when you send a message into the void and do not receive an immediate reply. This is a habit of the synchronous world that you must unlearn. You must trust the process, trust your team, and become comfortable with the quiet, focused space you have created for yourself.

The payoff for mastering this art is immense. Asynchronous communication is the operational framework that enables true freedom. It allows you to design your day around your life, not the other way around. It liberates you from the tyranny of the notification and the endless distraction of your inbox. It fosters a more inclusive work environment where the most thoughtful idea wins out, not necessarily the one from the loudest person in the room. By replacing the frantic, shallow chatter of the synchronous world with a calmer, deeper, and more intentional rhythm of collaboration, you unlock not only a more productive way of working, but a more balanced and sustainable way of living.

CHAPTER TWENTY-ONE: Scaling Your Business and Career from Anywhere

You've done it. The initial, frantic scramble is over. You have successfully untethered your professional life from a fixed location. You have a steady stream of income, a comfortable workflow, and a system for navigating the logistical hurdles of a life in motion. You are no longer just surviving as a digital nomad; you are stable. But with stability comes a new, more ambitious question. What's next? The skills that got you here—the hustle, the self-discipline, the ability to do great work from a laptop—are the skills of a successful solo operator. The skills that will take you to the next level are entirely different. This is the challenge of scaling.

Scaling is the intentional process of moving beyond the linear relationship between your time and your income. It is the transition from simply funding your travels to building significant wealth, from being a skilled practitioner to being a strategic leader. For the freelancer, it is the journey from a "business of one" to an agency. For the remote employee, it is the climb from an individual contributor to a management or leadership role. For the entrepreneur, it is the evolution from a founder who does everything to a CEO who directs a self-sufficient organization. This chapter is about that evolution. It is about understanding that the ultimate form of freedom is not just choosing where you work, but designing a career or a business that can grow far beyond your own individual capacity. It's about learning to build the machine, not just being a cog within it.

The journey begins with acknowledging the inherent ceiling of your current model. If you are a freelancer, your income is capped by the number of hours you can physically work and the rate you can command. You are the business, and when you stop, the income stops. If you are a remote employee, your career progression can be limited by a lack of visibility, a case of "out of sight, out of mind." To scale, you must fundamentally change your approach. You must shift your focus from doing the work to creating leverage. Leverage is the force multiplier for your efforts. It can come in the form of technology, of systems, of capital, or, most powerfully, of other people. The process of scaling is the process of strategically applying leverage to break through your current ceiling.

For the freelancer, the path to scaling is a journey up the value ladder. The first and most crucial step is to abandon the comfortable but limiting identity of a generalist. A generalist who "builds websites" or "writes articles" is a commodity, forced to compete on price in a crowded global marketplace. The first act of scaling is to specialize. You must carve out a specific niche where you can become the undisputed, go-to expert. This could be specializing in a particular industry (e.g., becoming the premier web developer for boutique wineries) or a particular skill set (e.g., the expert in email marketing automation for SaaS companies). This deep specialization allows you to solve a very specific, high-value problem for a very specific type of client. This is how you escape the pricing trap and begin to command premium rates based on your unique expertise, not just your time.

With this expertise established, the next step is to "productize" your service. Instead of selling your time in vague, hourly blocks, you package your solutions into clearly defined, fixed-price offerings. A freelance SEO specialist, for instance, might stop selling "SEO services" by the hour and start offering a "Startup SEO Launchpad" package. This package has a fixed price and includes a specific, predictable set of deliverables: a keyword research report, a technical site audit, and on-page optimization for ten core pages. This has a powerful psychological effect on the client. They are no longer buying your time; they are buying a tangible outcome. It simplifies your sales process, standardizes your workflow, and allows you to price your services based on the immense value you deliver, not the hours it takes you to do it.

This shift naturally leads to the final stage of the freelancer's evolution: moving from a doer to a strategist. As you become known for your expertise, clients will begin to seek not just your hands, but your brain. They don't just want you to execute the task; they want you to tell them what the task should be. The content writer becomes the content strategist. The social media manager becomes the digital marketing consultant. This is a profound leap in value. As a consultant, you are being paid for your strategic insights and your experience. This is the highest-leverage use of your time, and it is the foundation for the next phase of scaling: building a team.

You cannot build an agency if you are still spending your days on administrative tasks. Your first hire is almost always a virtual assistant (VA). This is your first act of true delegation. Conduct a ruthless audit of your work week. Identify all the low-value, repetitive tasks that are essential for running your business but do not require your unique expertise. This includes things like sending invoices, scheduling meetings, managing your inbox, and doing basic research. Delegating these tasks to a skilled VA is the single most powerful investment you can make in your own productivity. It frees up your time and mental energy to focus exclusively on high-value client work and on growing the business.

Once your administrative tasks are off your plate, you can begin to subcontract your core work. This is the birth of your agency. A freelance web developer might hire another developer to handle the coding for a project while they focus on the client strategy and project management. The key is to start small. Find reliable, high-quality contractors you can bring in on a project-by-project basis. This allows you to take on more work than you could handle on your own without the immediate overhead of a full-time employee. Your role now officially changes. You are no longer just a practitioner; you are a project manager. Your most important jobs are now quality control, client communication, and ensuring that the final product meets your high standards.

For the remote employee, the scaling journey is not about building a business, but about building a career. The primary obstacle is the lack of physical presence. You cannot rely on a chance encounter with a senior executive in the hallway to get noticed. Your path to promotion must be more deliberate, more documented, and more proactive than that of your office-based colleagues. Your greatest tool in this endeavor is to become an absolute master of asynchronous communication. Your written updates should be a model of clarity and conciseness. Your contributions in shared documents should be thoughtful and insightful. Your presence in the company's digital spaces should be so valuable that it becomes more powerful than any physical presence could be.

You must also shift from a passive, task-based mindset to one of proactive ownership. Do not wait to be assigned your next project. Actively look for problems, gaps in processes, and opportunities for improvement within the company, and be the one who proposes a solution. This demonstrates initiative and a commitment to the company's success that goes far beyond your job description. Volunteer for the challenging projects, the ones that are critical to the company's strategic goals. This is how you gain visibility and build a reputation as a problem-solver, not just a reliable pair of hands.

This visibility must be cultivated. You have to be intentional about building your internal network. Make a list of influential people in other departments and reach out to them for a brief, 15-minute "virtual coffee" chat. The goal is not to ask for anything, but simply to learn about their role and what their team is working on. This builds cross-functional relationships and gives you a broader understanding of the business. Be an active and helpful presence in the company's non-work-related Slack channels. Become known as a person, not just a name on an org chart.

As you do this great work, you must become your own public relations agent. Keep a private "brag document"—a running log of your accomplishments, complete with hard data and quantifiable results. It is not enough to say you "improved the website." You must be able to say you "led the redesign of the checkout flow, resulting in a 12% decrease in cart abandonment and a 5% increase in average order value in Q3." This document is the raw material you will use to build your case for a promotion or a raise during your performance reviews. It makes your contributions undeniable.

This culminates in the practice of "managing up." You cannot assume that your manager is aware of everything you are doing or that they are actively planning your career path. You must take control of this relationship. In your regular one-on-one meetings, come prepared with a clear agenda. This is your time to showcase your wins, discuss your challenges, and, most importantly, talk about your future. Ask direct questions: "What are the key skills I need to develop to move to the next level?" or "I'm interested in gaining experience in project leadership. Are there any upcoming opportunities where I could take on a bigger role?" This transforms your manager from a simple supervisor into an active partner in your career growth.

For the entrepreneur, scaling is the ultimate challenge. It is the process of transforming a business that is built around you into a valuable, self-sustaining asset that can run without you. The first and most critical step is to escape the "founder's trap," the belief that no one can do a task as well as you can. To scale, you must make yourself redundant in the day-to-day operations of your business. This is a process of systematization. You must extract the knowledge from your head and turn it into a set of documented processes that anyone can follow.

This is the creation of your company's playbook. Every recurring process, from how you onboard a new customer to how you publish a social media post, must be documented as a Standard Operating Procedure (SOP). This playbook is what allows you to hire someone and have them deliver a consistent, high-quality result without your constant oversight. Paired with this is a ruthless commitment to automation. Identify every repetitive, manual task in your business and find a piece of software that can do it for you. This could be using an email marketing platform to automate your sales funnel or using a tool like Zapier to create automated workflows that connect the different apps you use. Every process that is documented and every task that is automated is a brick in the foundation of a scalable business.

With these systems in place, you can begin to build your team. The transition from hiring contractors to making your first full-time hire is a major milestone. It comes with new legal and financial responsibilities, such as payroll and benefits, and it requires a significant investment of time and capital. Your first hires should be in roles that directly free you up to work *on* the business, rather than *in* it. This might be a customer support manager to handle all client communication or a project manager to oversee your team of contractors.

As you build this team, your style of leadership must evolve. You must learn to delegate outcomes, not just tasks. Instead of telling your new marketing hire exactly which social media posts to write, you give them the strategic goal: "Our objective for this quarter is to increase website traffic from social media by 20%." You then give them the autonomy, resources, and trust to figure out the best way to achieve that outcome. This is how you attract and retain top talent and build a team that is capable of innovating and solving problems on its own.

This growth will also necessitate a more formal business structure. The sole proprietorship that served you well in the beginning may no longer be adequate. You will likely need to incorporate your business, perhaps as a Limited Liability Company (LLC) or a similar entity in your home country. This protects your personal assets from business liabilities and can offer significant tax advantages. This is a complex area where professional legal and accounting advice is not just recommended; it is essential. An investment in a good international accountant is an investment in the long-term health and viability of your growing enterprise.

Finally, scaling requires a mental shift in how you view the money your business generates. In the early days, the profit was your salary, the fuel for your travels. As you scale, you must begin to see profit as fuel for the business itself. It is the capital you will use to reinvest in growth—in a more sophisticated marketing campaign, in better software, or in hiring another key team member. This is the transition from building a lifestyle to building an asset. A lifestyle business is a wonderful thing, but a scalable business is a valuable asset that you can one day sell, providing a level of financial freedom that a simple income stream never could.

Whether you are a freelancer building an agency, a remote employee climbing the corporate ladder, or an entrepreneur building a global company, the principles of scaling are the same. It is a journey away from the immediacy of doing and towards the leverage of designing. It requires you to let go, to trust others, and to shift your identity from that of a skilled practitioner to that of a strategic leader. This journey of professional growth is the second great adventure of the nomadic life, a challenge that can be just as rewarding and transformative as the act of exploring the world itself.

CHAPTER TWENTY-TWO: Handling Unexpected Challenges on the Road

For all the meticulous planning, the carefully crafted budgets, and the well-organized digital toolkits, there is an unwritten law of the road: at some point, something will go spectacularly wrong. A life of constant motion is a life of increased variables, and an increase in variables inevitably leads to an increase in unforeseen complications. Your flight will be cancelled. Your laptop will decide to die in a country where the keyboard layout looks like an alien script. You will get a stomach bug so debilitating that you begin to question all your life choices. This chapter is your emergency handbook, your guide to navigating the inevitable chaos.

It is crucial to understand that these moments are not a sign that you have failed or that the lifestyle is not for you. They are, in fact, an integral and unavoidable part of the journey. A smooth, flawless trip is a vacation. A nomadic life is an adventure, and adventures are defined by their obstacles. Your success as a long-term nomad will be measured not by your ability to avoid these challenges, but by the calm, resourcefulness, and resilience you bring to solving them. Think of this chapter not as a catalog of fears, but as a toolkit for building the confidence to handle whatever the world decides to throw at you.

Let's begin with the scenarios that can send a cold spike of adrenaline through even the most seasoned traveler: the loss of your essential documents and gear. Your passport, your wallet, and your laptop form the trinity of your nomadic existence. The loss of any one of them can feel like a catastrophic failure. The key to navigating this is to have a pre-planned, automatic response, a mental checklist that you can execute even when you are in a state of panic.

The undisputed king of travel disasters is a lost or stolen passport. The moment you realize your passport is gone, your first action is to file a police report. Go to the nearest police station and report the theft or loss. Be patient, be polite, and use a translation app if necessary. This police report is a critical document. It is often required by your country's embassy to issue a new travel document and is essential for any travel insurance claim.

Your second, simultaneous action is to locate the nearest embassy or consulate for your home country. A quick Google search will give you the address, hours, and phone number. Call them immediately to report the loss and ask for instructions. Most embassies have a specific process for issuing an emergency passport to stranded citizens. This is a limited-validity document designed to get you home or allow you to continue to your next destination where you can apply for a full replacement. To facilitate this process, you will need to prove your identity. This is where your preparation pays off. Having a digital copy of your passport's photo page, your birth certificate, and any other form of government-issued ID stored securely in the cloud is invaluable. You will also need new passport photos, which can typically be taken at a small photo shop near the embassy. The process can take anywhere from 24 hours to a few days, so be prepared for a delay in your travel plans.

A lost or stolen wallet presents a more immediate, though less bureaucratic, crisis. The moment you realize your cards are gone, you must act with speed to mitigate the financial damage. Find a secure internet connection and log into your online banking apps. Most banks now have a feature that allows you to instantly freeze or cancel your cards directly from the app. If this is not an option, you need to find the international helpline number for your bank— a number you should have saved in your phone and in a secure digital note—and call them to cancel everything.

Once your cards are neutralized, you face the problem of having no money. This is where your system of redundancy becomes your lifeline. Your backup debit and credit cards, which you wisely stored in a separate location from your main wallet, are now your primary financial tools. If your entire collection of cards was taken, you will need to access emergency cash. One of the most reliable ways is to have a family member or trusted friend send you money via a service like Western Union or Remitly. They can send the funds online, and you can pick up the cash at a local agent's office, usually within minutes, using a form of identification. It is a slightly stressful and expensive process, but it is a reliable bridge to get you through until your replacement cards can be shipped to you.

Perhaps the most professionally devastating event is the loss, theft, or sudden death of your laptop. Your entire business resides within that metal shell. The first step, if it has been stolen, is security. Use your phone to access your device's "Find My" feature to remotely lock and, if necessary, erase the hard drive. This protects your sensitive client data and personal information. The second step is to enact your backup plan. Because you have been maintaining a continuous cloud backup and a periodic backup to a portable SSD, your work itself is not lost. This is a moment of profound relief that makes every dollar and every minute you spent on your backup strategy worthwhile.

The logistical challenge is now replacing the hardware. This can be a complex undertaking in a foreign country. Finding a reputable electronics store is your first task. Be wary of a deal that seems too good to be true. Research the local market to understand fair pricing. Be prepared for practical differences; a new laptop might come with a different keyboard layout (such as QWERTZ in Germany or AZERTY in France), which can take some getting used to. Also, understand that your warranty may not be international. A new Apple device will likely be covered globally, but the warranty for a PC brand might only be valid in the country of purchase. In some cases, the most efficient solution might be to buy a cheap, temporary tablet or Chromebook to tide you over while you arrange for a friend or family member to ship you a new machine from your home country.

Beyond the loss of physical items, health emergencies are another major source of on-the-road stress. Waking up with a raging fever or taking a fall on a cobblestone street is scary enough at home; in a foreign country, it can feel terrifying. Your first port of call in a non-life-threatening situation should be your travel medical insurance provider. Their 24/7 assistance line is staffed by professionals who can assess your situation and refer you to a reputable, English-speaking doctor or a pre-approved clinic in their network. This simple phone call can save you a world of stress and uncertainty.

In a more serious emergency, your priority is to get to the nearest hospital. You can find this information on Google Maps, or by asking your hotel staff or Airbnb host. Do not delay seeking care out of fear of the cost; your health is more important. Once you are stable, you or a travel companion should contact your insurance provider as soon as possible. They will need to be informed of your hospitalization to coordinate with the medical staff and arrange for payment. Be prepared for the possibility that you may have to pay for some services upfront with a credit card and submit the receipts for reimbursement later. This is another reason why having a high-limit credit card and a healthy emergency fund is so critical.

The language barrier can feel particularly daunting in a medical context. A translation app on your phone is an essential tool for communicating your symptoms and understanding a doctor's instructions. It is also helpful to have the generic, scientific name of any allergies or chronic conditions written down, as these are more internationally recognized than brand names. Remember that medical professionals around the world are dedicated to helping people, and they will almost always find a way to communicate and provide you with the care you need.

Sometimes the challenge is not a dramatic event, but a slow-burning logistical nightmare. You might miscalculate your visa-free days and find yourself in a country illegally. This is a serious situation. Do not ignore it or hope that no one will notice. The consequences of overstaying a visa can range from a hefty fine to deportation and a multi-year ban. Your best course of action is to seek professional advice immediately. A quick online search for an immigration lawyer in your current city can provide you with a consultation to understand your options, which might include paying a fine upon departure or applying for an extension.

Accommodation disasters are another common frustration. You arrive at your month-long rental only to find that it is filthy, the Wi-Fi doesn't work, or it is located next to a construction site that starts drilling at 6 AM. This is where booking through a platform with strong consumer protections is vital. If you have a problem with an Airbnb, for example, your first step is to document everything. Take photos and videos of the issues. Then, contact the host through the platform's messaging system to give them a chance to resolve the problem. If they are unresponsive or unhelpful, you should immediately contact the platform's customer support and invoke their protection policy. They can often help you find alternative accommodation and secure a refund.

Professional crises do not stop just because you are in an exotic location. You might lose your biggest client, or your remote company might announce a round of layoffs. This can feel like the ground has disappeared from beneath you. The first step is to take a deep breath and not panic. This is precisely why you built your Freedom Fund. That financial buffer gives you the breathing room to absorb the shock without having to immediately book a flight home. It allows you to spend the next few weeks not in a state of desperation, but in a focused, strategic search for your next opportunity.

You might also be the source of the crisis. A travel delay could cause you to miss a critical deadline, or a misunderstanding could lead to a major mistake on a client project. The way you handle this professional failure is a true test of your character. The worst thing you can do is to hide or make excuses. The best thing you can do is to communicate immediately, honestly, and proactively. Own the mistake, explain the situation concisely, and, most importantly, come with a plan to fix it. This level of professionalism and accountability can, paradoxically, end up strengthening a client relationship more than if the mistake had never happened at all.

To prepare for any of these potential disasters, it is wise to create a "digital emergency kit." This is a secure folder in your cloud storage that contains copies of all your essential documents: your passport, your driver's license, your birth certificate, the front and back of all your credit and debit cards, your travel insurance policy, and a list of emergency contact numbers. Having all this information in one easily accessible place can be a lifesaver in a crisis.

Ultimately, handling unexpected challenges on the road is about building the muscle of resilience. Each problem you solve, from navigating a foreign pharmacy to finding a last-minute flight, is a rep in your resilience training. It proves to you, again and again, that you are more capable and more resourceful than you thought. While these moments are deeply stressful in the short term, they are often the source of your greatest growth and your best stories in the long term. No one ever tells a captivating story about the time their trip went exactly as planned. It is in the chaos, the confusion, and the eventual triumph over adversity that the true adventure lies.

CHAPTER TWENTY-THREE: The Journey Home: Managing Reverse Culture Shock

There is a final, unwritten chapter to every grand adventure, one that begins not with the thrill of a boarding pass, but with the familiar click of a key in your own front door. For the digital nomad, the journey home is often the most complex and emotionally turbulent leg of the entire trip. You have spent months, perhaps years, mastering the art of adaptation, learning to navigate foreign cultures with grace and resilience. You arrive home expecting a sense of relief, a comfortable return to the familiar. Instead, you are blindsided by a disorienting and deeply unsettling feeling: the realization that the most foreign country you have visited all year is the one you used to call home.

This phenomenon is known as reverse culture shock. It is not simply a case of post-travel blues or a nostalgia for the open road. It is a genuine and often profound psychological disorientation that occurs when you return to your native culture after an extended period abroad. The world you left behind seems to have remained frozen in time, while you have undergone a fundamental transformation. The familiar has become strange, and the values and routines you once took for granted now seem arbitrary and baffling. For many, reverse culture shock is a far more challenging experience than the initial culture shock of moving abroad, precisely because it is so unexpected. You are prepared for things to be different in Bangkok; you are not prepared for things to feel different in your own kitchen.

The experience often begins with a short and deceptive "honeymoon" phase. The first few days or weeks are a joyful reunion with the creature comforts you have missed. You revel in the simple pleasures of a hot shower with consistent water pressure, the ease of finding your favorite brand of peanut butter at the grocery store, and the deep comfort of sleeping in your own bed. It is a period of relief, a welcome respite from the constant low-grade stress of navigating a foreign environment. Your friends and family are thrilled to see you, and you are the center of attention, regaling them with your most exciting tales from the road.

This initial euphoria, however, is almost always fleeting. It soon gives way to a creeping sense of frustration and irritation. The very things you were excited to return to begin to grate on your nerves. The conversations, which at first felt so comforting, start to seem superficial. Your friends listen politely to your stories for a few minutes, but their eyes quickly glaze over. They cannot truly comprehend the experience of navigating a Moroccan souk or the feeling of watching the sunrise over a volcano in Guatemala. Their concerns soon revert to the familiar topics of local sports, office politics, and home renovations. It is not that they do not care; it is simply that your lived reality has become an abstraction to them.

This is the crisis stage of reverse culture shock, and it is where the real struggle begins. You start to view your own culture with the critical eye of an outsider. The rampant consumerism, the obsession with productivity, the traffic, the political discourse— things you never questioned before—now seem absurd and exhausting. You find yourself making constant, unfavorable comparisons. You might lament the lack of walkable cities compared to Europe, or miss the vibrant street food culture of Southeast Asia. You begin to idealize your life abroad, your memory conveniently filtering out the visa frustrations, the loneliness, and the constant scramble for good Wi-Fi. You remember only the breathtaking sunsets and the exhilarating sense of freedom, creating a romanticized past that your present reality cannot possibly compete with.

This can lead to a profound sense of alienation. You feel like an actor playing a part, going through the motions of a life that no longer fits. You are surrounded by the people you love most in the world, yet you feel completely and utterly misunderstood. This dissonance can trigger a genuine identity crisis. On the road, your identity was clear: you were the traveler, the nomad, the adventurer. Back home, that identity is stripped away. You are no longer defined by your mobility and your global perspective. You are just... back. This feeling of being an outsider in your own home is the lonely, paradoxical heart of reverse culture shock.

Navigating this transition requires acknowledging that you are not the same person who left. Travel has irrevocably changed you. It has broadened your perspective, challenged your assumptions, and reshaped your priorities. The goal is not to somehow revert to your old self, but to find a way to integrate your new, expanded self into your old environment. This is a slow and deliberate process of readjustment, a conscious effort to build a new life that honors the person you have become.

The first step in this process is to manage your own expectations, ideally before you even get on the plane home. Understand that your return will be challenging. Acknowledge that reverse culture shock is a real and well-documented phenomenon. Knowing what to expect can strip the experience of its power to blindside you. Recognize that while you have been on a grand adventure, your friends and family have been living their own lives, with their own triumphs and struggles. Their world did not stop while you were away, and you cannot expect them to be as invested in your journey as you are.

When you do arrive, give yourself permission to go slow. Resist the pressure to fill your calendar with a frantic series of catch-up coffees and reunion parties. The constant social performance can be draining. You need time to decompress, to process the end of a major life chapter, and to simply be still. Your body and mind need time to adjust to a new rhythm. Treat your return with the same gentleness and self-compassion you would afford to someone recovering from a long illness. It is okay to say no to social invitations. It is okay to spend a Saturday doing nothing at all.

One of the most powerful strategies for bridging the gap between your traveler self and your at-home self is to become a tourist in your own town. You have spent months exploring new cities with a sense of wide-eyed curiosity. Apply that same mindset to your hometown. Visit that museum you have always meant to go to. Hike a local trail you have never explored. Try that new restaurant in a neighborhood you rarely visit. This simple act of exploration helps to reframe your home not as a boring, static place, but as a location with its own potential for discovery. It reminds you that adventure is a mindset, not a location.

You must also find your new tribe. While your old friends are a vital part of your life, they may not be the right audience for your deepest reflections on your travels. Seek out other people who have had similar experiences. Use platforms like Meetup.com or search for local expat or traveler communities online. Finding someone you can talk to who will nod in recognition when you describe the specific frustration of trying to open a bank account in a foreign language is an incredibly validating experience. These are the people who will truly "get it," and their companionship can be a powerful antidote to feelings of isolation.

As you readjust, you will need to find a way to share your experiences without overwhelming or alienating your friends and family. The key is to become a better storyteller. Instead of giving a long, chronological account of your trip, learn to share small, relatable anecdotes. Instead of saying, "Thailand was amazing," tell a specific, funny story about your attempt to order street food using only hand gestures. Instead of talking broadly about cultural differences, connect your experience to something they can understand. When a friend complains about their commute, you can share a story about the beautiful chaos of scooter traffic in Hanoi. The goal is to build a bridge between your two worlds, not to simply broadcast from the other side.

It is also critical to stay connected to the global community you built on the road. Your relationships with other nomads and friends you made abroad are a vital part of your new identity. Do not let these connections fade. Schedule regular video calls. Maintain your group chats. These relationships are a living reminder that the person you became on the road is still who you are. They are a link to a part of your life that is real and ongoing, even if it is physically distant. Knowing that you have friends scattered across the globe can make your hometown feel less like a final destination and more like a temporary base of operations.

A common challenge upon returning is the sudden lack of purpose. The nomadic life is filled with a constant stream of short-term goals: finding a new apartment, navigating a new city, planning your next border crossing. A settled life can feel strangely aimless by comparison. To combat this, you need to find a new project, a new challenge to channel your energy into. This could be anything from signing up for a language class or a new fitness regimen to starting a creative project or volunteering for a local cause. Having a goal to work towards provides a sense of forward momentum and helps to fill the void left by the constant stimulation of travel.

You must also find ways to incorporate the best parts of your nomadic lifestyle into your new, more stationary reality. Did you love the simplicity of living with fewer possessions? Use your return as an opportunity to declutter your home and commit to a more minimalist lifestyle. Did you discover a love for a particular type of cuisine? Make a point of learning to cook it at home. Did you appreciate the daily walk to a local café? Build that ritual into your new routine. These small, conscious acts are a way of honoring your experience and refusing to let the lessons of the road fade away.

Be prepared for the emotional rollercoaster. There will be days when you feel a profound sense of grief for the life you left behind. This is normal. You are mourning the loss of a period of intense growth, freedom, and adventure. Allow yourself to feel that sadness without judgment. Journaling can be an incredibly powerful tool for processing these complex emotions. Writing down your thoughts and feelings can help you to make sense of the disorientation and to find clarity amidst the confusion.

It is also important to recognize that your return home does not have to be a permanent sentence. For many nomads, a trip home is a strategic "pit stop." It is a chance to reconnect with loved ones, to work without the distraction of travel, and to save money for the next adventure. The experience of reverse culture shock, while challenging, can be a powerful diagnostic tool. It shines a bright light on what you truly value. It helps you to see your own culture with fresh eyes, to appreciate its strengths, and to identify the parts that no longer align with who you are.

This period of readjustment is a journey in itself. It will test your patience and your self-awareness. It can take months, and sometimes even a year or more, to feel fully integrated and at peace. Be kind to yourself during this process. The disorientation you feel is not a sign that you have made a mistake. It is the mark of a life well-lived, the inevitable and beautiful growing pain that comes from having a heart and a mind that are now big enough to call more than one place in the world home.

CHAPTER TWENTY-FOUR: The Future of Work: Trends in Remote and Hybrid Environments

The global, unplanned experiment in remote work that began in the early 2020s was not the beginning of a revolution, but its sudden and dramatic acceleration. The seeds of a location-independent workforce had been quietly sprouting for over a decade, nurtured by advancements in technology and a growing desire for a more flexible and autonomous professional life. The pandemic did not invent the concept; it simply forced the entire world to confront its viability, shattering decades of corporate dogma in a matter of weeks. As the dust has settled, it has become clear that this was not a temporary detour, but a permanent fork in the road. The office, as a mandatory daily destination, has lost its monopoly on professional life. We are now in the midst of a great realignment, a period of experimentation and evolution that is actively shaping the next century of work.

For the digital nomad, this evolving landscape presents both immense opportunity and new complexities. The lifestyle is moving from a niche pursuit for a handful of pioneers to a mainstream, globally recognized way of working. Understanding the major currents of this transformation is no longer just a matter of intellectual curiosity; it is a critical skill for navigating your career and making strategic decisions about your future. The trends emerging today—in corporate policy, in technology, and in government—are the signposts pointing to where the world of work is heading. Reading them correctly will be the key to staying ahead of the curve and ensuring the long-term sustainability of your location-independent life.

The most immediate and widespread trend to emerge from the global work-from-home experiment is the hybrid model. For a vast number of companies, a full return to the traditional five-day-a-week office became an untenable proposition, met with fierce resistance from employees who had tasted a new kind of freedom. At the same time, many leaders remained hesitant to embrace a fully remote workforce, citing concerns about culture, collaboration, and the perceived value of spontaneous, in-person interaction. The hybrid model emerged as the great compromise, a middle ground attempting to offer the best of both worlds.

This model, however, is not a monolith. It exists on a wide spectrum of flexibility. At the more rigid end is the "structured hybrid" approach, where the company dictates which specific days employees must be in the office, for example, every Tuesday through Thursday. A slightly more flexible version is the "at-will" model, where employees have a set number of in-office days per week or month that they can schedule as they see fit. At the most progressive end of the spectrum is the "remote-first" hybrid model. In this setup, the company operates as if it were fully remote, with asynchronous communication as the default. The office is treated not as a mandatory workspace, but as an optional resource, a "clubhouse" for intentional, in-person collaboration, team-building events, or focused work away from home.

For the aspiring nomad, the rise of the hybrid model is a double-edged sword. On one hand, it has dramatically increased the number of "remote-friendly" jobs available, normalizing the idea that work can happen outside the office. On the other hand, it can create a new kind of tether. A company that requires employees to be in a specific office three days a week is not offering location independence; it is offering a slightly more flexible commute. This has created a new challenge for remote workers: proximity bias. This is the unconscious tendency for managers to favor the employees they see every day in the office. The in-person worker who can grab a coffee with the boss is often more visible and top-of-mind than the remote employee who is just a face on a screen, which can lead to disadvantages in mentorship, project assignments, and promotions.

While the hybrid model has become the dominant choice for many large corporations, a growing and influential cohort of companies is taking a more radical leap, embracing a permanent "Work from

Anywhere" (WFA) policy. These are the true pioneers of the future of work, organizations that have fundamentally decoupled their operations from a physical headquarters. For these companies, the decision is not a mere employee perk; it is a core business strategy. By committing to a WFA model, they unlock the single greatest advantage in the modern economy: access to a truly global talent pool. A software company based in San Francisco is no longer limited to hiring engineers who can afford to live in the Bay Area; they can hire the best possible engineer for the job, whether that person lives in Bangalore, Buenos Aires, or Berlin.

This strategy also offers significant financial benefits. The astronomical costs associated with prime downtown office real estate—rent, utilities, maintenance, security—are drastically reduced or eliminated entirely. These savings can be reinvested into other areas of the business, such as research and development, or passed on to employees in the form of higher salaries and better benefits. Companies like GitLab, which has been fully remote since its inception and has hundreds of employees in dozens of countries, have become the standard-bearers for this model, proving that it is possible to build a highly successful, multi-billion-dollar enterprise without a single physical office. As more companies prove the viability of this model, the pressure will mount on others to follow suit in order to compete for top talent.

This global talent war has ignited one of the most contentious debates in the remote work world: the issue of location-based pay. As companies begin hiring from a global talent pool, they are forced to confront a complex question: should a software developer in Ohio be paid the same salary as a developer doing the exact same job in New York City? The arguments on both sides are passionate. Many companies contend that salaries should be adjusted based on the local cost of living and market rates, arguing that paying a San Francisco salary to someone in a low-cost location would be an inefficient use of capital. They often establish a series of regional pay bands, with compensation adjusted based on a "geo-index."

On the other side, a growing number of employees and remote-first advocates argue for location-agnostic pay. Their position is that compensation should be based on the value of the work and the skill of the individual, not on their geographic location. They argue that it is unfair to penalize an employee for choosing to live in a more affordable area. Some progressive companies have adopted this model, establishing a single, global pay scale for each role, often pegged to a high-cost market like San Francisco or New York. For the digital nomad, this is a trend of profound importance. A job that offers location-agnostic pay is the ultimate enabler of geoarbitrage, allowing you to maximize your savings and quality of life. Conversely, a role with a strict geo-indexing policy might limit your travel options or require you to take a pay cut if you decide to move to a more affordable country.

This global distribution of workers is being enabled by a tsunami of new technology designed specifically for the remote and hybrid world. The first generation of remote work tools, like Slack and Zoom, were primarily focused on replicating the communication patterns of a physical office. The next wave of technology is far more ambitious, aiming to create entirely new modes of collaboration that are native to the digital realm. The most hyped of these is the concept of the "metaverse office," using Virtual Reality (VR) and Augmented Reality (AR) to create immersive, three-dimensional virtual workspaces. Instead of seeing your colleagues as faces in a grid on a screen, you would interact with their digital avatars in a shared virtual environment, allowing for a more natural sense of presence and spatial awareness. While still in its early stages, this technology has the potential to solve some of the persistent challenges of remote collaboration, such as spontaneous brainstorming and the organic building of social rapport.

Alongside these immersive platforms, the development of Artificial Intelligence (AI) is set to fundamentally reshape the remote work experience. AI-powered assistants are already capable of automating many of the tedious administrative tasks that consume a significant portion of the workday. They can automatically transcribe meetings, generate concise summaries, and identify key action items. They can manage complex scheduling across multiple time zones, draft routine emails, and even assist with research and data analysis. As these tools become more sophisticated, they will act as a powerful force multiplier for the individual worker, freeing up cognitive bandwidth to focus on the high-level strategic and creative tasks that humans do best.

This technological evolution is driving a deeper cultural shift toward a truly asynchronous-first way of working. Companies are realizing that the goal is not to be "always on," but to create systems that allow work to progress smoothly around the clock, without constant real-time check-ins. This has led to the rise of a new generation of sophisticated project management and documentation platforms. These tools are designed to be the "single source of truth," a central, shared brain for the entire organization. They integrate task management, long-form documentation, and threaded conversations in one place, creating a rich, contextual record of every project. This level of documentation is the bedrock of an effective async culture, allowing anyone to get up to speed on a project at any time, from any time zone.

As companies and workers have gone global, governments have begun to wake up to the reality of this new world order. The rise of the digital nomad visa, once a niche offering from a few small countries, has become a global trend. Nations are now in direct competition with each other to attract this new class of mobile, high-earning professionals. They recognize that a digital nomad is the ideal visitor: they spend their foreign-earned money in the local economy, supporting restaurants, cafés, and tourism, all without taking a job from a local citizen. We can expect to see this trend accelerate, with more countries launching visa programs, streamlining their application processes, and offering more attractive incentives, such as preferential tax rates, to lure remote talent.

This governmental adaptation will likely extend beyond visas. The current legal and tax frameworks in most countries are built on a twentieth-century model of a fixed employer in a fixed location.

They are ill-equipped to handle the complexities of a global, distributed workforce. In the coming years, we can anticipate the slow but steady evolution of international agreements and tax treaties designed to accommodate this new reality. This could lead to the creation of a new legal status for the location-independent worker, a kind of "global remote worker" classification that would simplify tax obligations and provide a clearer set of rights and responsibilities.

This transformation is also forcing a fundamental re-evaluation of what constitutes company culture. When culture is no longer defined by a shared physical space, a ping-pong table, and free snacks in the kitchen, what is it? The most forward-thinking companies are discovering that remote culture must be built with a level of intention and deliberation that was never required in an office. It is a culture built on a foundation of trust, transparency, and exceptionally clear written communication.

To foster the human connection that is essential for a thriving team, the new model of "office time" is the company off-site or retreat. Instead of seeing each other every day for mundane tasks, teams are brought together a few times a year for focused, high-value, in-person events. These gatherings are not for day-to-day work; they are for the activities that are genuinely better in person: strategic planning sessions, deep-dive workshops, and, most importantly, social bonding. This model of periodic, intentional gathering combined with deep, focused remote work is proving to be a powerful formula for building strong, cohesive, and highly effective teams.

This evolving landscape demands a new set of skills from the modern professional. The most successful remote workers of the future will not be the ones who are best at replicating their office habits at home. They will be the ones who master the unique competencies of the distributed work environment. Exceptional written communication will no longer be a "nice to have" skill; it will be the absolute, non-negotiable foundation of professional life. The ability to convey complex ideas with clarity, precision, and the right tone in a written format will be the primary determinant of your influence and effectiveness.

Alongside communication, the skill of radical self-management will be paramount. Without the external structure of an office, you must become the CEO of your own productivity. This requires a deep understanding of your own work rhythms, the discipline to create and stick to your own routines, and the ability to manage your time and attention in a world of infinite digital distractions. In a remote environment, your career progression is entirely in your hands. You must be the proactive driver of your own visibility, the architect of your own internal network, and the chief advocate for your own professional development.

The digital nomad lifestyle, born from a desire for personal freedom, now finds itself at the very center of the global conversation about the future of work. The trends are clear: work is becoming more flexible, more distributed, and more asynchronous. The rigid structures of the industrial age are giving way to a more fluid, trust-based, and output-focused model. This is not a future that is decades away; it is a reality that is being built, tested, and refined in real-time. For the individual who is prepared to embrace this new world—the one who can master the tools, cultivate the skills, and adapt to the evolving landscape—the promise is not just the freedom to travel, but the opportunity to build a richer, more integrated, and more deeply human way of working and living.

CHAPTER TWENTY-FIVE: Thriving, Not Just Surviving: Creating a Sustainable and Fulfilling Nomadic Life

You have reached the final chapter of this handbook, and if you have journeyed through these pages with intention, you are armed with a formidable arsenal of practical knowledge. You have the tools to land a remote job, the strategies to navigate a foreign tax system, and the wisdom to pack your entire life into a 40-liter bag. You know how to survive. This chapter, however, is not about survival. It is about the subtle, challenging, and profoundly rewarding art of thriving. Survival is a state of maintenance, of getting by. Thriving is a state of growth, of deep engagement, and of genuine, sustainable fulfillment.

The initial motivation for this lifestyle is often a powerful push away from something: the soul-crushing commute, the rigid nine-to-five, the feeling of a life unlived. This initial burst of energy is enough to get you through the first six months, or even the first year, on a wave of novelty and adrenaline. Every new city is a puzzle to be solved, every new dish a discovery. But eventually, the novelty fades. The logistics of finding an apartment and a good Wi-Fi connection become routine. The constant travel can start to feel less like an adventure and more like a job in itself. This is the moment when the real journey begins. It is the point where you must transition from a life defined by what you are running from, to a life defined by what you are building towards.

To thrive as a digital nomad in the long term, your "why" must evolve. The initial escape is a valid and powerful catalyst, but it is not a sustainable fuel. You must find a deeper purpose, a reason for being on the road that transcends the simple act of not being at a desk. This requires a period of introspection, of asking yourself the hard questions. What kind of life are you trying to build? What experiences are you seeking that truly nourish you? What kind of person do you want to become through this process? The answers to these questions will become your new compass, guiding your decisions and providing a resilient sense of purpose when the initial excitement wanes.

One of the first and most critical strategic shifts in the journey from surviving to thriving is the conscious decision to slow down. In the beginning, there is a powerful temptation to engage in a kind of frantic "country collecting." You might plan to spend one month in each city, a whirlwind tour of the globe designed to maximize the number of pins on your map. While exhilarating, this pace is the single most common cause of nomadic burnout. The constant logistical overhead of finding new housing, navigating new transport systems, and establishing new routines every thirty days is emotionally and mentally exhausting. It keeps you perpetually in the shallow end of a new culture, always an observer, never a participant.

The antidote to this is the practice of "slowmadism." Slow travel is not about being lazy; it is a deliberate strategy for sustainability and depth. It means choosing to stay in one place for three months, or six, or even a year. This extended timeframe dramatically reduces the stress of constant transit. More importantly, it allows you to move beyond the superficial tourist experience and begin to build a genuine, albeit temporary, life. You have the time to find your favorite local café where the barista knows your order. You can join a gym or a language class, creating a routine and a community. You have the breathing room to form friendships that go beyond a single shared meal.

This slower pace is also a financial superpower. By committing to a longer stay, you unlock access to the local rental market, which is almost always significantly cheaper than the monthly rates on short-term platforms. You have the time to figure out the most affordable way to shop for groceries, to use public transport like a local, and to discover the hidden gems that are not listed in the guidebooks. Slow travel transforms a destination from a product to be consumed into a community to be inhabited. It is the difference between a life of constant transit and a life of deep, immersive experiences.

As you slow down, you begin to discover that a sense of "home" is not something you have to give up to live a nomadic life. It is something you learn to carry within you. While a fixed address may be a thing of the past, a sense of stability is a fundamental human need. The key to thriving on the road is to become a master at creating this stability for yourself, building a portable sense of home that is independent of your geographical location. This is a practice built on routine and ritual.

These rituals are the anchors in your sea of constant change. They can be as simple or as complex as you need them to be. It could be the non-negotiable ritual of starting every single day with fifteen minutes of meditation or journaling, an act that grounds you in your own mind before you engage with the outside world. It could be the physical ritual of fully unpacking your suitcase the moment you arrive in a new apartment, the simple act of putting your clothes in a drawer signaling to your brain that this is a place of rest. It could be a work ritual, like the "shutdown routine" we discussed, that creates a firm boundary between your professional and personal life.

These routines extend to your weekly and monthly cadence. Perhaps every Sunday is your "life admin" day, where you pay your bills, plan your week, and call your family. Maybe the first day of every month is your financial review day. This predictable rhythm creates a comforting scaffold of normalcy, a sense of control and order amidst the inherent unpredictability of the lifestyle. It is this internal structure that allows you to handle the external chaos with grace. You learn that "home" is not a place, but a state of being that you can cultivate and carry with you, no matter where you lay your head.

With this internal stability in place, you can begin to tackle the complex relationship between your work and your life. The traditional concept of "work-life balance" is often a poor fit for the digital nomad. It implies a rigid separation, two distinct spheres that must be kept in a delicate equilibrium. For a nomad, these spheres are not separate; they are deeply and inextricably intertwined. The goal is not a perfect balance, but a healthy and intentional integration. Your work is the engine that enables your travels, and your travels are the source of the inspiration and perspective that enriches your work.

This integrated life requires a new level of intentionality and a fierce commitment to boundaries. Without the physical separation of an office, it is dangerously easy for work to become a low-grade hum that is always on in the background. You might find yourself checking emails while in line at a museum or taking a client call from a scenic viewpoint. This constant context-switching means you are never fully present in either your work or your leisure. You are doing a mediocre job of working and a mediocre job of experiencing the world.

The solution is to be as deliberate about scheduling your life as you are about scheduling your work. When it is time to work, you work. You find your quiet space, you turn off your notifications, and you give your full, focused attention to the task at hand. When it is time to live, you live. You physically close your laptop, you put your phone on silent, and you immerse yourself completely in the experience in front of you. This might mean declaring certain days of the week as "no-work exploration days." It might mean setting a hard rule that you never open your laptop after 6 PM or on weekends. These boundaries are not limitations; they are the structures that allow you to be fully present and engaged in every aspect of your rich, multifaceted life.

As you practice this integrated life over the years, you will find that your needs and desires begin to evolve. The nomadic journey is not a static state of being; it is a dynamic arc. The frenetic, budget-conscious, hostel-hopping style that defined your first year on the road may feel exhausting and unfulfilling by year three. You may find yourself craving more comfort, more stability, and deeper community connections. This is a natural and healthy evolution, and the beauty of this lifestyle is its infinite adaptability.

For many long-term nomads, this evolution leads to a hybrid model. They might choose to establish a "home base" in a city they love, a place where they have a long-term lease, a stable community, and a place to store their belongings. They might spend six to nine months of the year at this base, living a more settled life, and then use the remaining months for more focused travel. Others may transition to a life of part-time nomadism, spending a season or a specific part of the year abroad and the rest at home. Some nomads find a partner on the road and evolve into a nomadic couple, navigating the unique joys and challenges of a shared adventure. Others still may become "nomad families," adding the complexities of schooling and childcare to their mobile lives.

There is no single correct path. The key is to be honest with yourself about your changing needs and to give yourself permission to redefine the lifestyle to fit your current stage of life. The goal is not to be a "digital nomad" in the purest, most dogmatic sense of the term. The goal is to design a life that brings you joy and fulfillment. If that means trading in a backpack for a lease, that is not a failure; it is a successful adaptation.

This personal evolution will also change how you measure success. In the beginning, it is easy to fall into the trap of a nomadic vanity metric. You might find yourself subtly competing with other nomads on the number of countries you have visited or the number of stamps in your passport. This is the traveler's equivalent of keeping up with the Joneses. It is a shallow and ultimately unfulfilling game. A thriving nomad learns to abandon this external scorecard and to create their own.

Your new definition of success might be measured in skills learned, not miles traveled. It could be the fluency you gain in a new language, the mastery of a new professional competency, or the development of a creative talent like photography or cooking. It might be measured in the depth of your relationships, not the breadth of your itinerary. One genuine, lasting friendship forged in a new city is worth more than a dozen fleeting acquaintances. It might be measured in your contributions, in the positive impact you have on the communities you visit. It is a deeply personal and qualitative assessment, a shift from asking "How much have I seen?" to "How much have I grown?"

This brings us to one of the most powerful catalysts for a fulfilling nomadic life: the shift from a consumer to a contributor. A life spent simply consuming new sights, new foods, and new experiences can, over time, begin to feel hollow. A deep and lasting sense of purpose often comes from giving back, from using your unique skills and privileged position to make a positive contribution to the communities that host you. This is the final step in the journey from being a guest to becoming a true global citizen.

This contribution can take many forms. It could be structured, formal volunteering with a local non-profit organization. It could be informal skill-sharing, offering to teach a free workshop on digital marketing at your co-working space or helping a local artisan set up a simple e-commerce website. It could be as simple as committing to a regular beach clean-up or participating in a local community event. These acts of service, no matter how small, create a powerful sense of connection and purpose. They transform your relationship with a place from a transactional one into a reciprocal one. You are no longer just a visitor taking from a community; you are an active participant giving back to it.

Ultimately, a thriving, sustainable, and fulfilling nomadic life is built on a foundation of unglamorous, consistent work. It is the daily practice of checking in with yourself, of honoring your physical and mental health above all else. It is the intentional effort you put into nurturing your most important relationships, both near and far. It is the courage to constantly redefine your own version of success and to adapt your lifestyle to meet your evolving needs.

This handbook has provided you with a map, a detailed guide to the practical terrain of this extraordinary lifestyle. But a map can only show you the path. The journey itself is yours to walk. It will be filled with moments of breathtaking beauty and periods of profound challenge. There will be days of exhilarating freedom and nights of quiet loneliness. It will not always be easy, but it will be yours. You have been given the rare and precious opportunity to be the architect of your own life, to build a reality that is as vast and as varied as the world itself. The tools are in your hands. The adventure awaits.

www.ingramcontent.com/pod-product-compliance
Lightning Source LLC
LaVergne TN
LVHW051335050326
832903LV00031B/3556